"Whereas most communication advice is concerned with what to say or even how to say it, *Magic Words* places the focus where it belongs: on the other person. Tim David offers keen insight into how to better connect with others in business and in life." —Adam Grant, Wharton professor and *New York Times* bestselling author of *Give and Take*

"As an author, I believe the words we choose to use are everything. They impact our relationships, goal achievement, and happiness. Tim David understands the power of using the right words. In this practical book, David gives us specific ways and tools to simply make everything better in our lives." —John G. Miller, author of *QBQ!*, *Outstanding!*, and *Parenting the QBQ Way*

"The magician's art seems obvious once we deconstruct it—and Tim David's seven words appear obvious until he takes them apart to show us their secrets, deftly teaching us how to create our own magic. Perhaps it's not surprising that I found the book persuasive, entertaining, and . . . mesmerizing!" —Rosalie Maggio, author of *How to Say It*

"Magicians notice the little things—and count on the rest of us to *not* notice them, to make the magic happen. In this book, Tim David pulls back the curtain to reveal the stunning power of everyday words when used the right way. This is a fascinating book, filled with strong science and compelling stories, and a must-read for anyone who deals with other humans on a regular basis." —Heidi Grant Halvorson, author of *9 Things Successful People Do Differently* and associate director of the Motivation Science Center, Columbia Business School

"Fresh, simple, and on target! In every interaction, we increase or decrease trust. Mr. David gets it! He gives a clear blueprint for building connections and transforming relationships using seven powerful words! This is one book I will use! Thank you." —David Horsager, bestselling author of *The Trust Edge*

continued . . .

"I have spent decades teaching people how to make deeper connections with one another. I am happy to report that Tim David's *Magic Words* will help you do this simply, quickly, and easily. Put Tim's suggestions into everyday life, and you too will believe there is real magic and influence in the power of words. Prove it to yourself by reading this now."
—Kenton Knepper, author of *Wonder Words*, mentalist, suggestion expert, and sound influencer

"*Magic Words* stands out from the clutter of communication books pushing tired clichés. Tim David offers fresh, intelligent insights on the art and science of motivating and influencing human beings. If you work with people, you'll want this book." —Joel Bauer, international speaker and author of *How to Persuade People Who Don't Want to Be Persuaded*

"*Magic Words* is a fantastic book because it not only explains the science behind why certain words can trigger an automatic response, but also shows you how you can use those words to motivate friends, colleagues, and even yourself. If you can imagine a small shift in the way that you use some common words resulting in lots more people doing what you ask them to do, then you are already seeing the results that you can get from *Magic Words*." —Rintu Basu, international bestselling author of *The Persuasion Skills Black Book*

"Words are powerful. *Magic Words* helps you understand and apply that power. A fun and practical read, the book will give you a different perspective on your word choices, helping you choose the right words at the right time." —Nick Kolenda, author of *Methods of Persuasion*

"Every once in a while you read a book that is rich with ideas and concepts you can immediately apply to get dramatic results. Putting the principles Tim has shared into practice can take you from effective to highly influential. This is a must-read for everyone, not just salespeople, because after all communication and influence are essential components of your personal and professional life." —Ken Cheo, president of Our Sales Coach

"Because of today's technology most of us are staring at an iPhone or a tablet screen to communicate. Tim David's magic words will teach you how to build stronger human connections with anyone you interact with. Throughout the years, David's words have always been inspiring. Now . . . everyone can take advantage of his mastery."

—Nathan Kranzo, television magic consultant

"Most people think the financial industry is a knowledge business. This is *not* a knowledge or numbers business—you give me an iPad and the Internet and I can figure out just about anything. This is now a *words* business, a *language* business, a *questions* business, and a *stories* business. Want to increase your productivity? Work on your words, language, questions, and stories! Tim David is able to articulate the proper words for any industry and this book is a great resource to improve *your* words and language."

—Tom Hegna, economist and author of *Paychecks and Playchecks*

"As someone who speaks from the stage, my job is to carefully select each and every word for maximum impact. Tim David's book, *Magic Words*, gives a thorough insight in to some of the most psychologically charged words that any of us can utter. Through a series of anecdotes and metaphor-riddled tales, Tim gives us so much more than definitions. Instead, we leave with deep understanding of not only context but also the cold, hard science behind the use of these specially chosen 'magic words.'"

—Kennedy "That Mind Reader Guy," multi-award-winning corporate event entertainer

"We always knew that sticks and stones may break our bones, and now we know exactly what words do to the human brain. Great book!"

—Scott Barry Kaufman, scientific director of the Imagination Institute and a researcher in the Positive Psychology Center, University of Pennsylvania

"In a time of social media, texting, emails, and people hiding behind screens, I highly applaud *Magic Words* as a powerful read of simple words that, when used right, inspire greatness—not just within you, but others as well. This book is a welcomed gust of wind to a very concerned up-and-coming generation of young adults." —Jeff Yalden, America's #1 teen motivational speaker, and celebrity teen and family life coach

continued . . .

"Educators, counselors, and all those in the helping professions will find life-changing wisdom in *Magic Words*. Tim David's insightful observations on life and truly powerful communications practices are presented in an entertaining page-turner that breathes fresh air into strategic learning. The busiest teachers, counselors, and marketing professionals must take the time to read this outstanding, joyous, magical book."

—Dr. Guy D. Alba, principal at St. Margaret School, Rumford, RI, and adjunct professor in the School of Professional Studies (Masters in Counseling Program), Providence College

"Tim David accurately translates social psychological research into seven powerful principles that can help people better communicate with others. These simple tricks from a master magician show that words matter because connection matters." —Sara Konrath, director of the Interdisciplinary Program for Empathy and Altruism Research, Lilly Family School of Philanthropy, Indiana University

"If you're interested in becoming more ethically powerful, having people say yes to you more often, or just needing to become more persuasive and influential, then *Magic Words* is an essential addition to your library. Tim David has created a book filled with easy-to-follow advice, strategies, and tactics that you want and need. Get it." —David M. Frees III, JD, author, attorney coach, and "The Grand Master" of persuasion and influence skills

"*Magic Words* is hands-down the single most definitive and important resource about how to influence, persuade, motivate, and connect with people, using language alone. Everyone on earth should have this book on their shelves if they want to become a more compelling, engaging, and influential speaker, friend, adviser, salesperson, or business owner. If you want to become naturally powerful and persuasive, you *must* read *Magic Words*. It's like a real-life book of spells!" —Rob J. Temple, hypnotist and lifestyle coach

"Quick, useful, and fascinating. Tim David has collected seven of the most powerful words English has to offer. Understand them and you'll understand people." —Geoff Ronning, cofounder of StealthSeminar.com and business consultant

MAGIC WORDS

The Science and Secrets
Behind 7 Words That Motivate,
Engage, and Influence

Tim David

PRENTICE HALL PRESS

PRENTICE HALL PRESS
Published by the Penguin Group
Penguin Group (USA) LLC
375 Hudson Street, New York, New York 10014

USA • Canada • UK • Ireland • Australia • New Zealand • India • South Africa • China

penguin.com

A Penguin Random House Company

MAGIC WORDS

ISBN: 978-0-7352-0539-0

An application to register this book for cataloging has been submitted to the Library of Congress.

First edition: December 2014

PRINTED IN THE UNITED STATES OF AMERICA

10 9 8 7 6 5 4 3 2 1

Text design by Tiffany Estreicher

Most Prentice Hall Press books are available at special quantity discounts for bulk purchases for
sales promotions, premiums, fund-raising, or educational use. Special books, or book excerpts,
can also be created to fit specific needs. For details, write: Special.Markets@us.penguingroup.com.

CONTENTS

We know that words cannot move mountains, but they can move the multitude. . . . Words shape thought, stir feeling, and beget action; they kill and revive, corrupt and cure. The "men of words"—priests, prophets, intellectuals—have played a more decisive role in history than military leaders, statesmen, and businessmen.

—Eric Hoffer, *The Ordeal of Change*, 1976

THE BIGGEST PROBLEM IN THE WORLD

There is a problem we find in our governments, in our schools, and in our families. It affects every country in the world and every citizen in them. We invest years of our lives and billions of dollars in an attempt to solve it. Big companies battle it. Non-profits dread it. Entrepreneurs study solutions to it. In fact, it's taunting me right now as you read this. It's big. It's everywhere. And I don't see it going away on its own anytime soon.

HERE ARE SOME EXAMPLES OF IT...

- Teachers can't get their students to do their homework.
- Managers can't get their team members to work harder or more efficiently.
- Interrogators can't get their subjects to speak the truth.
- Salespeople can't get their prospects to buy more products.
- Doctors can't get their patients to comply with treatment plans.

- Parents can't get their kids to behave.
- Entrepreneurs can't get investors to buy in to their vision.
- Nonprofit organizations can't get people to donate to a cause.
- Poker players can't get their competition to bet big.
- Religious leaders can't get people to convert.
- Negotiators can't get their opponents to make concessions.

The biggest problem in the world?

Not being able to get people to do stuff.

Solve this problem and you can solve anything. If more parents could motivate their children and effectively lead them into adulthood, if more teachers could inspire and engage their students, if more doctors could influence their patients toward greater health, then this world would be a better place.

To do anything of any significance on this planet, you need an army. If you want to create lasting change or do "real and permanent good," as Andrew Carnegie espoused, then you need to motivate a movement. I don't care if you want to start a business, or a nonprofit organization, or a family. It doesn't matter if you want to make a movie, write a book, or go to Mars. You can't do it alone. It's pretty hard to be a leader if no one is following. If you want to move mountains, then you need to be able to move people.

THE STANDARD SOLUTIONS

Most people try to motivate others by begging, bribing, and reasoning them to death. When that doesn't work, they get desperate and start nagging, manipulating, or deceiving to get the results they want.

They believe that "getting to yes" is the only goal of their communication. In reality, that's not good enough. Not only do we want people to say "yes" to us, but we want them to follow through and DO what they promised.

This is a book about words that turn into action. It's about motivating employees, engaging students, starting movements, empowering children, helping customers, and becoming an influential leader. In short, it's about getting people to do stuff.

Kind of.

I should start right away with the big secret of getting people to do stuff. It's simple and yet paradoxical.

You *can't*.

Getting people to do stuff is the *goal*, not the process. If you try to motivate people directly, you will fail. Anyone who has ever tried to change someone's behavior knows this to be painfully true.

As best-selling author Daniel Pink says, "Motivation is not something we do to other people." The old adage goes, "You can lead a horse to water, but you can't make him drink." However, *you can make him thirsty*.

Motivation and influence are about creating conditions where the human brain becomes "thirsty" in such a way that the body follows. The great news is that the vast majority of brains are already thirsty in some way. They are going through life with a series of wants, needs, and desires. You just have to drill down, find their motivation, and tap into it. When you do that, watch out! Your biggest problem will not be generating motivation, but directing it.

The seven magic words in this book aren't just words. Their

roots touch the deep needs that every person has. Saying "be-cause" is about establishing purpose. Saying "yes" displays accep-tance. Using a person's name shows significance. These are deeply human drives that we all share. They connect us.

In order for any communication to get results—whether it's a magic trick I'm performing on the stage, or a sales pitch you're giving in the boardroom—it must begin with an elusive little thing called human connection.

Human connection is the soil where "getting people to do stuff" grows. Get this piece right and you can mess up in a lot of other areas and still get results. Get this piece wrong and the game is over before you've even begun.

When teachers are truly connected with their students, learn-ing happens. When doctors are truly connected with their patients, healing happens. When companies are truly connected with their customers, business happens.

A SKILL IN CRISIS

While the quantity of human interaction has been skyrocketing, the quality of human connection has been dissolving.

Social psychologist Sara Konrath believes that it's no coinci-dence. Her research numbers are shocking.

A growing number of studies . . . over the past three decades have found decreases in empathic concern (i.e., sympathy for the mis-fortunes of others) along with increases in narcissism.

This pattern of decreasing empathy and increasing self-centeredness has led us to a situation where "getting people to do stuff" is all about us and our own motivations instead of about them and *their* motivations. It's no wonder we've gotten so bad at it.

So the greatest problem in the world requires the greatest solution in the world: an immediate and widespread increase in human connection.

And words are a darn good place to start.

A WORD ABOUT WORDS

In 1967, UCLA professor Albert Mehrabian published two now-famous research papers that made a very bold claim. Only 7 percent of what we communicate to others has anything to do with the words that we say; the rest is transmitted through our vocal tone and body language (38 percent and 55 percent, respectively).

The phrase "It's not what you say, it's how you say it" has since reached cliché status. Over the last five decades, "experts" have been brandishing this statistic as a means of selling their books or getting you to attend their body language seminars. This concept has been all but beaten into our heads—and often by people who don't fully understand what the original study actually found.

If you believe their interpretation of Mehrabian's study, then you should be able to watch a show in Spanish and understand 93 percent of what is going on from vocal tone and body language alone—even if you don't speak Spanish!

It doesn't work that way.

Here's what Mehrabian himself said: "Unless a communicator is talking about their feelings or attitudes, these equations are not applicable."

This explains why non-Spanish-speaking people can watch a Spanish TV show and accurately perceive the emotions that the characters are portraying.

However, words aren't completely devoid of emotion either. As psychologist John Gottman points out, "Plays would not exist if words did not contain a great potential for communicating emotional information."

And mastering words is an even more important skill in a time when emails and texts have taken over a significant percentage of our interactions.

So who's right? Is what you say more important than how you say it, or vice versa? Does it depend on the situation?

Actually, it's the wrong question.

What you say isn't *necessarily* important. How you say it isn't *necessarily* important. Even the intent behind what you say isn't *necessarily* important either.

So stop worrying about all that stuff. It's not about you anyway. Instead, start focusing on what people *hear*. Rather than look at percentages, we need to start looking at the overall *effect* that our communication has on the people we share it with.

How language affects people—that's the true magic of words.

> [It] wasn't language itself. It wasn't the utterance of language itself. It wasn't even what somebody meant. But it's how that language affected me.
>
> —Walter Mosley, "Let That Weight Go," TheMoth.org

YOUR LAZY BRAIN

Your brain loves shortcuts. The world is a complex place and your brain is being relentlessly assaulted with an incredible amount of sensory information. You've got to have a series of preprogrammed responses to help you deal with the deluge.

That's why when you hear a sudden loud noise, your body jolts to attention. When you see delicious food, your mouth waters. When the room is dark, hot, or both, you get drowsy. Automatically. You don't have to think, it just happens.

Like Pavlov's dogs, we experience these conditioned responses because our brain has learned to anticipate what's coming next. Some of these lessons are programmed into our brains through thousands of repeated life experiences. Some are preprogrammed deeper into our brains through hundreds of thousands of years of our ancestors' experiences.

Is it possible that there are similar "cause-and-effect" responses happening in our brain when we hear certain words? Is it possible that there are certain pieces of human communication that universally command a very specific "shortcut" reaction?

Yup.

It is also possible to intentionally cue up those reactions in the brains of those around us in order to more effectively communicate. You see, the words discussed in this book are not merely buzzwords or catchphrases. They don't depend on the listener's status or upbringing. (In some cases, it doesn't even matter if the person *is* listening.) They lose none of their potency when translated into other languages, and they are unaffected by cultural shifts. The phenomenon created by these magic words is a deeply *human*, instinctive response.

You now know something that 90 percent of the population either doesn't fully understand or refuses to accept.

Whenever you speak, you're affecting the brain of anyone who hears you. If you choose not to speak, your silence affects them. Your communication changes their very neurochemistry.

The people who refuse to accept this do so because they are afraid of being *manipulative.* Some don't like the idea of influencing other people's thoughts for supposed ethical reasons, and some just don't want the responsibility. However, in order to be an effective communicator, you must embrace this fact: whether you intend to or not, you are manipulating the thoughts, feelings, and actions of others.

Don't worry, you're in good company. Here are some of the great manipulators of history: Mother Teresa, Abraham Lincoln, Martin Luther King Jr., Winston Churchill, Maya Angelou, Gandhi, Eleanor Roosevelt, and countless others who have used the people-moving power of words to ignite human rights movements, free slaves, empower the weak, and bring about political reform. They are great communicators, yes, but manipulators?

When we think of manipulation, we think of the not-so-great manipulators of history. People like Bernie Madoff, Frank Abagnale Jr., Benny Hinn, or anyone else who uses the same exact skills to sell bad used cars, acquit guilty defendants, or con the elderly out of millions. But in reality, both groups influenced the thoughts, emotions, and actions of lots of other people.

The difference, then, is in intention. No one doubts that communication is a powerful tool. And just like physical tools, communication can be used to build up or tear down. In the hands of Paul Bunyan, an ax is a helpful tool. In the hands of Lizzie Borden, it is a deadly weapon. It's not the ax itself; it's the *intent* of the person using the ax.

The rest of this book will provide you with powerful tools. Before using any of them, give yourself the "public relations test." Ask yourself: "What would happen if this conversation were recorded and picked up by every major news outlet? How would the public feel about my intent? Would 95 percent of people agree that what I'm doing is the right thing?" When our intent is questionable, we tend to want to hide in the shadows. When our intent is positive, we have no problem shouting it from the rooftops.

Fortunately, most of us aren't like Lizzie Borden. If you're the type of person who would read a book like this, then I doubt your intention is to hurt other people with your words. Instead, the real danger for us comes when we end up like Chris Hanson.

In 2003, Chris Hanson was the punter for the Jacksonville Jaguars. Head coach Jack Del Rio tried motivating Chris and the rest of his team by placing a huge tree stump in the locker room along with an ax. Players were encouraged to hack away at the log a little bit each day in order to illustrate the value of persistence. "Keep chopping wood" was the metaphorical mantra.

Sometime around the fifth week of the NFL season, Hanson took a hack at the log and missed. Instead, he took a hunk out of his leg. So serious were his injuries that he was immediately rushed to the hospital for emergency surgery. Fortunately, Chris Hanson recovered and was able to continue punting footballs for the Jaguars.

In this case, the ax wasn't really used as a tool and it wasn't really used as a weapon. It was a powerful tool in the hands of an unskilled craftsman. That's the dangerous middle ground where damage gets done and people get hurt. It's the same with communication. It is a powerful tool, but all too often it is wielded by unskilled craftsmen.

People love to "wing it" when communicating. In most situations, they follow their impulses and react to every whim. They just grab the ax, take a swing, and hope they hit log and not leg. They might as well put on a blindfold first. It's okay to go off the grid and wing it every once in a while with your communication, but you should only break the rules if you've learned them first. In the field of acting, the best ad-libbers are those who know the script inside and out.

With that in mind, let's take a look at our first magic word and see the powerful effects it has on the minds of all who hear it.

"YES"

I was kneeling in the cold and dusty gravel by my car, holding something small and hoping for something big. This time, there would be no magic tricks. No clever psychology or jokes—just a simple question.

"Will you marry me?"

Silence.

More silence.

It didn't happen this way when I was rehearsing it over and over in my mind. My stomach started doing flips as worst-case-scenario thoughts raced through my mind. *She hates the ring! My proposal wasn't romantic enough! She's repulsed by the idea of spending the rest of her life with me!*

Oh great, now she's crying.

I hadn't planned for this.

She seemed lost for words, so I mustered two awkward sentences.

"So, are you gonna answer? My knees are kinda starting to hurt."

That's when the dam broke.

"YES!"

She flung her arms around me and pressed sobs of joy into my shoulder.

To this day, it is the most magical word I have ever heard.

The marriage relationship is a beautiful thing—and a wonderful place to learn about human interaction. Perhaps there is no one who has studied it more than Dr. John Gottman. Thousands of married couples have visited Gottman's "Love Lab" to have their interactions documented on film and analyzed.

Decades of research has given Gottman an uncanny ability to predict divorce. According to his studies, after observing any married couple for as little as five minutes, he can predict (with about 91 percent accuracy) which couples will be divorced and which couples will still be together fifteen years from now. That's impressive stuff—even to a magician. It appears that Dr. Gottman has cracked the code of human relationships.

He looks for six signs of divorce. Any one of them left unchecked can ruin a marriage. Five out of the six are rooted in the exact opposite of what "yes" represents. His most notorious example is the expression of contempt. Along with criticism, defensiveness, and stonewalling, contempt makes up Gottman's "Four Horsemen of the Apocalypse"—his second indicator of divorce.

Much worse than just saying no to an idea, contempt is a "no" directed right at the heart of the other person. It's a complete rejection of who they are. It's saying, "I am morally superior to you."

According to legendary nonverbal communication expert

Paul Ekman, a contemptuous sneer is the single most dangerous human facial expression we can make—worse than disgust or even rage. It is the only naturally asymmetrical facial expression, and it has been shown to cause physical, bodily harm to anyone who sees it.

Think about that. When you express contempt to others, you're affecting not only their emotions or their minds, but their physical bodies! Their blood pressure and heart rate increase and their immune system begins to break down. In fact, according to Gottman, "Couples who are contemptuous of each other are more likely to suffer from infectious illnesses than other people."

Contempt is the exact opposite of what "yes" represents, and that's why it destroys human relationships of any kind—even marriages bound by vow and law.

Another example is Gottman's fifth sign of divorce, what he calls "failed repair attempts." This is when one spouse tries to connect with their partner during an argument. It could be an apology, a gesture, or some other reminder that they're on the same team. When the other spouse says no to that repair attempt and maintains (or increases) their anger or negativity, it increases the likelihood of divorce.

"That's why I can predict a divorce by hearing only one discussion between a husband and wife. The failure of repair attempts is an accurate marker for an unhappy future. The presence of the four horsemen alone predicts divorce with only an 82 percent accuracy. But when you add in the failure of repair attempts, the accuracy rate reaches into the nineties."

Nothing is more heartbreaking than to see someone extend olive branch after olive branch to their spouse, only to have them thrown back in their face.

The good news is that while "no" can destroy relationships, "yes" can bring them together. Six of Gottman's "7 Principles for Making Marriage Work" essentially revolve around saying yes with your words and actions. In a chapter titled "Let Your Partner Influence You," Gottman builds a case that accepting influence actually makes you more influential. In other words, saying yes encourages people to say yes back to you.

"Yes" bridges conflict, fosters admiration, creates shared experience, and offers acceptance. Within a marriage relationship, "yes" is clearly a magic word with impressive power. With it, marriage succeeds. Without it, marriage fails. Decades of research has shown this to be true with 91 percent accuracy.

Does the power of "yes" carry over to other kinds of human relationships?

In a word, yes.

THE PSYCHOLOGICAL SIGNIFICANCE OF A SIMPLE "YES"

We fear rejection.

The haunting question "What if they say no?" has prevented sales calls from being made, pay raises from being requested, and women from being asked out for as long as there have been people on this planet to worry about such things.

Survey after survey confirms the number one fear among people is the fear of public speaking—otherwise known as the fear of public rejection. As a species, we've learned that crowds should be around us, not directly in front of us. There is safety in numbers, and when we experience rejection of any kind, we lose that safety net. A primitive but very powerful part of our brain perceives rejection as a threat to our very survival. "No" hurts like nothing else.

A "yes," on the other hand, is the exact opposite of rejection. It's a sign of acceptance, of understanding, and of positivity. It means we don't have to change (we HATE to change). Our brains love hearing it. That's why volumes have been written solely on the topic of how to get more people to say yes to us. We crave it deeply.

It's obvious that "yes" is a magic word of the highest order. Let's look at how we can use it to positively motivate, engage, and influence.

ASK YOURSELF POSITIVE OUTCOME QUESTIONS AND ANSWER "YES"

Before delivering a presentation, a salesperson might ask himself positive outcome questions that sound like this:

- Am I going to deliver a compelling pitch?
- Are they likely to buy from me?
- Will they be satisfied with their purchase?

As it turns out, the very act of asking the questions is magical. In their fascinating paper "Motivating Goal-Directed Behavior through Introspective Self-Talk: The Role of the Interrogative Form of Simple Future Tense," researchers Ibrahim Senay, Dolores Albarracín, and Kenji Noguchi describe the surprising results of a clever experiment they conducted in 2010.

Participants were led to believe that the researchers were "interested in people's handwriting practices" and asked to write one of the following four words or phrases twenty times: "I," "Will," "Will I," or "I will." Once the writing task was completed, they were given a series of word puzzles to solve. The group that wrote the interrogative phrase "Will I" outperformed all three other groups in the word-puzzles task by nearly double.

It appeared that priming the subjects with a question instead of a statement significantly improved their performance on a subsequent task. Three more related experiments substantiated this even further.

This is why *To Sell Is Human* author Daniel Pink recommends adopting cartoon favorite Bob the Builder's famous approach. In each episode, Bob is presented with a problem, and instead of spouting possible solutions, he switches to interrogative mode by asking, "Can we fix it?"

That's good advice. However, there is also a second half of Bob's incessantly optimistic credo—"Yes we can!" Embedded front and center is our magic word "yes." The optimism this "yes" carries brings an added magic all its own. A study done by Peter Schulman, published in the *Journal of Selling and Sales Management*, found that salespeople who are optimistic outsell their pessimistic counterparts by 35 percent.

The defining trait of an optimist is that they'll answer positive outcome questions with a "yes." Pessimists, on the other hand, prefer to stick with the go-to answer they use for just about everything—"no." This puts them at a significant disadvantage.

However, pessimists needn't despair (although they would probably prefer to). Martin Seligman, author of *Learned Opti-*

mism and a renowned psychologist and clinical researcher, has been studying optimists and pessimists for more than twenty-five years. He states, "Pessimism is escapable."

But even if your pessimism refuses to believe that, try taking a look into the past. In a study by Adam Galinsky and Thomas Mussweiler of the Institute of Psychology at the University of Würzburg, negotiation participants who were told to "remember a time when you felt dominant or powerful" just before the negotiation, tended to wield more influence over the early stages of the negotiation process, and they ultimately achieved better individual outcomes.

There is an element of the "fake it till you make it" principle at play here. Even if you don't feel too positive about the outcome, say yes anyway. Your brain creates deep associations between the word "yes" and the positivity, optimism, and confidence required to be a more influential communicator. Just by saying it, your brain remembers all the times you said yes in the past. Usually great things were happening. For example, when your favorite team scored a goal you likely shouted, "YES!" If someone offered you a particularly delicious dessert, you replied with a yes. Feelings of excitement, positivity, optimism, and confidence seem to follow the word "yes" wherever it goes.

You can enhance this effect on your brain by getting your body involved, too. Say yes with a confident tone of voice and perhaps a little more volume than usual. Pump your fists in the air. Nod your head while wearing a confident smile. Clap your hands together. I dare you to try it right now and not feel more confident.

Oprah Winfrey has famously used this technique. She was staring at a twelve-foot-long bed of 1,000-degree burning coals, and self-help guru Anthony Robbins told her to walk across it barefoot. She wasn't having any of it: "Oh NO! You're kidding me. This is crazy. All mammals know to run from fire!"

"What's the worst that could happen? Burn your feet off and die? Come on!"

What happened next was powerful, yet so simple that you might miss it. Consider his next words carefully. This is the most famous motivational speaker on planet Earth. He has countless techniques at his disposal for motivating people. How did he choose to influence quite possibly the single most influential woman of our time?

He got her to motivate herself by using this one simple technique. He said, "I want you to scream 'yes!' I want you to do it three times, and I want you to storm across."

By this point the rhythmic chanting had begun. Hundreds of people were clapping their hands, pumping their fists in the air, and chanting to the beat of a tribal drummer, "YES! YES! YES!" over and over again. Oprah took a deep breath, screamed "YES!" three times as loud and as strong as she could, and then confidently marched across the blazing embers unharmed. The crowd went wild.

To be clear, I am absolutely not saying that the word "yes" was the reason she was not burned. The reason she wasn't burned had everything to do with plain physics and a trained staff. It had nothing to do with the words coming out of her mouth.

What saying the word "yes" did was allow Oprah to call up those positive, confident associations when she needed them most. Taking the first step is all about confidence level (or "state," as Robbins refers to it), and the word "yes" magically and instantly puts you in just the right state for walking across coals (or selling a product, or negotiating a raise).

In addition to saying yes to yourself before an interaction in order to boost your influence power, there is a specific time when you should be saying this magic word to the people you hope to move to action.

FIND THE FIRST "YES"

During every argument, negotiation, sales pitch, performance review, or platform presentation, you should strive to find a "yes" early on. There is always something you can both say yes to. Don't be afraid to be the one who says yes first.

Saying yes at the beginning of an interaction eases tension, creates rapport, and opens minds.

Sometimes you don't even have to express this acceptance verbally. In fact, your body language can go a long way in the beginning of an interaction. When someone first encounters you, their brain does a quick "threat assessment." It searches for clues in an attempt to answer the question "Can I trust you?" Your posture, your eye contact, your handshake, your feet, your overall tone, and the rest of your nonverbal cues should all be screaming back the message, "Yes!"

So smile! Adopt an open body posture. Face them directly and lean slightly forward. Maintain solid eye contact (without staring). Mirror their actions. Don't ever point at anyone, don't cross your arms, and don't let your nose get too high in the air. Following these simple rules of body language will help you pass any threat assessment with flying colors. The "yes" that you say with your body will make the other person feel an instant sense of rapport with you.

For more in-depth body language training and videos, visit MagicWordsBook.com/body.

GREAT "YESWORK" IN ACTION

Sally works at a gym and she's about to meet with potential member Eric. They both know that membership is in Eric's best interests, but he is resistant. See how Sally masterfully uses "yes" to help him overcome his hesitations:

SALLY: *(smiling and friendly)* Hi, are you Eric?

ERIC: Yes.

SALLY: Great! You're here for your ten-thirty appointment, yes?

ERIC: Yep.

SALLY: I can't believe it's only ten-thirty! It's way too hot out there to be ten-thirty in the morning.

ERIC: *(Smiles and nods.)*

SALLY: Well, we're glad you braved the heat wave. What brings you in today?

ERIC: Well, I think it's about time I get in shape.

SALLY: Yes, and you've come to the right place!

ERIC: Well, that's what I'm trying to figure out. I've got some other options to look at still.

SALLY: But you're here! Obviously, there's a good reason for that?

ERIC: You're the closest gym to my house.

SALLY: Yes, and we have five hundred other locations worldwide, too. Obviously, a gym membership doesn't do you any good if you don't ever go, right?

ERIC: Yeah, I've gone down that road before.

SALLY: But somehow I get the feeling this time is totally different for you. Tell you what, let me give you a tour, and then we'll come back here and I'll show you some numbers.

ERIC: Okay, sounds good.

Eric wants to get in shape, and now he's got the best chance of that actually happening, thanks to Sally's excellent communication skills. Let's break this down and see exactly why Sally said the things she said.

THE "LITTLE YESES"

Sally didn't make the mistake of going for the big "yes" first. Instead, she went for the "little yeses."

You'll notice that Sally seemed to waste time in the beginning of her conversation with Eric with a bit of apparent small talk. That small talk was actually very intentional and surprisingly magical.

A study of a group of salespeople revealed the power of getting "little yeses." The study looked at whether or not getting someone to say yes during a conversation would affect the outcome of that conversation.

First, the salespeople went about their business as usual. They were able to close 18 percent of the sales—not bad. However, when they were instructed to get a minimum of three "little yeses" early on in the conversation, suddenly they were able to close 32 percent of the sales. Sounds like a magic word to me.

So what exactly is this mysteriously powerful "little yes"? Quite simply, it's anytime someone says yes to you—*any*time. It doesn't matter how small the agreement is, as long as they're agreeing with you. If you look back, you'll see all the "little yeses" in Sally and Eric's conversation.

The first one was a positive response to the question "Are you Eric?" Even that one counts! Sally continues, "You're here for your ten-thirty appointment?"

"Yep."

That's two! A "yep" is not exactly a "yes," but it's definitely on the same spectrum. Count it. Similarly, when he nods to her comment about the weather, that's another affirmative response we can count as a "little yes." Can a comment about the weather *really* help Sally get Eric to join her gym? It can, if it guides Eric toward a "little yes."

FIVE MORE WAYS TO ELICIT "LITTLE YESES"

Tag Questions

You'll see that Sally is a master of the tag question, *isn't she?* People are accustomed to agreeing to tag questions. If someone tags a question such as "right?" or "aren't you?" onto the end of a statement, it's very difficult to disagree with them. My personal favorite tag question is the magic word itself. You can see yourself using tag questions in your conversations today, *yes?*

You'll see a few examples above in the Sally and Eric conversation, but what you won't see is how Sally delivers the tag questions. They're written with question marks, but they're delivered as statements. She has a confident, authoritative tone of voice and—this is very important—there is no upward vocal inflection as she speaks them.

A variation on the tag question is the negative question. Phrasing a question this way—"Doesn't everybody want to get into shape?"—is more likely to get a positive response than phrasing it in the positive, "Does everybody want to get into shape?"

Both tag questions and negative questions are most effective when delivered as statements. Add some to your conversations and watch the little yeses start flowing.

LY-ing

There is nothing dishonest about LY-ing. Quite the opposite, LY-ing requires obvious, blatant truths. LY-ers start sentences with words like "obviously," "clearly," or "naturally." Certain words (that often end in "ly") have natural, built-in agreement. Who is going to disagree with something that's obvious? Not many people will, and those who do should be watched very carefully. Sally combined a bit of LY-ing with a tag question and it worked like a dream ("Obviously, a gym membership doesn't do you any good if you don't ever go, right?"). Chalk up another little yes.

Backtracking

Backtracking is not only a way to get another little yes, it's also a good listening skill. If Sally needed any more little yeses, she could have tried a backtracking question like "You said you've gone down that road before?" Eric can't do anything but give a little yes, because he just said that he's gone down that road before. The human brain does not like to disagree with itself.

One mistake many people make with backtracking is they confuse it with clarifying. Clarifying happens when you put someone's statements into your own words. Usually, you'll clarify because you have no idea what the other person is trying to say. So, in order to better understand, you clarify. You paraphrase their thoughts in your own words and repeat them back, usually preceded by a question like "Are you saying that . . . ?" or followed by ". . . is that right?"

You don't ever want to paraphrase while backtracking. Don't mess with their words. Say EXACTLY what they said to you. Don't paraphrase, "parrot-phrase." The secret is using their exact words without sounding like you're mocking them.

Imagine if Sally had paraphrased Eric's sentence and turned it into: "Oh, so you've failed before?"

Eric hadn't said anything about failing, and although "that road" means "failure" to Sally, it might mean something entirely different to Eric. Paraphrasing here is not likely to get the little yes that Sally is after. In fact, it might get her into trouble.

Noddables

Some statements can get just about anyone to nod in agreement. I call them "noddables": "It's better to be safe than sorry." "A bird in the hand is worth two in the bush." "It's better to give than to receive."

Sure, they sound cliché. Sure, everyone's heard them a thousand times. That's the point. They are bits of wisdom ingrained in a deep part of our collective subconscious, and whenever we hear them, we agree. It's like that song you hear on the radio six times per day. You may not have liked it at first, but it grew on you. The more we hear something, the more we like it. That's why old cliché statements so often result in agreement. We know what we like, and we like what we know.

Here's something interesting: if you are nodding your own head while delivering a noddable, the person you are speaking to is much more likely to nod themselves. This "monkey see, monkey do effect" has been observed for a long time. Recent discoveries in neuroscience confirm that our brains are wired for shared experience. There is even a special type of neuron, called a "mirror neuron," that is instrumental in generating this mimicry compulsion that you've likely experienced yourself. That's why yawns are often contagious. In fact, just reading the word "yawn" may call to mind a mental image of someone yawning. This imaginary person's yawn is probably big and wide, and I wouldn't be surprised if it makes you yawn sometime in the next ten seconds. Go ahead, try and fight it.

Barnum Statements

Fraudulent psychics are notorious for their use of Barnum statements. Named after P. T. Barnum (the "There's a sucker born every minute" guy), they are statements that are so general nobody can disagree with them:

> *At times you are withdrawn and quiet, while at other times you are outgoing and personable.*

This Barnum statement is a generalization that is true for everyone. Stranger still, it makes the listener feel like the speaker is talking specifically about them. Someone skilled in delivering Barnum statements can make people feel like they know them on a deep level. This is why it is a favorite technique of fraudulent psychics.

As for you, you probably won't be giving psychic readings. Instead, you're going after little yeses. Barnum statements are like compliments. You should only deliver them in an authentic, genuine manner. Let's say you're discussing a case study with a prospect. Here's how you might drop in an honest Barnum statement:

Now, this guy was rather shy. Actually, that's not true. He was like all of us. I'm sure at times you are withdrawn and quiet, while at other times you are outgoing and personable.

For a list of the top twelve most-agreed-with Barnum statements, visit MagicWordsBook.com/barnum.html.

"YES" MATCHING

Responding to every positive statement with "yes" is an incredibly powerful technique that I stumbled across years ago while reading an old newsletter about medical hypnosis. It is designed to build rapport and create more "yes" momentum. Don't overlook its power just because it's incredibly simple. Give it a try the next time you find yourself wanting to be persuasive.

In our example dialogue, every time Eric said something positive, Sally started her response with a "yes," or a "yes, and." (Never with a "yes, but.") Also, every time Eric said something negative, Sally began her response with a "but." (Look for more on the word "but" in the next chapter.)

THE DISAPPEARING NEGATIVES—WHAT ERIC NEVER HEARD FROM SALLY

Sally did not mention any other gyms, and she never put anyone down—a wise strategy. Instead of trying to get Eric to say no to her competition, Sally focused on getting him to say "yes" to her company. If she hadn't, then she'd have fallen victim to "disappearing negatives."

The emotional brain doesn't handle negative words very well. "No" or "not" are almost sure to disappear from your subconscious, resulting in you reacting exactly the opposite of the original intention. Here's a little experiment you can do right now to experience this effect firsthand:

Do not think of the word "rhinoceros" for the next ten seconds.

How did you do? It's quite difficult, isn't it? The more you try to push it out, the more it comes charging back to the forefront of your mind. That's because of the disappearing negative "do not." It's as though your brain only heard "Think of the word 'rhinoceros' for the next ten seconds."

Here are a few more real-life examples of the disappearing negatives effect:

- An airline pilot comes on the loudspeaker and says, "Ladies and gentlemen, this is your captain speaking. I just want to let you know that there is absolutely no cause for concern."—*How do you feel?*
- Your spouse comes home after a week away and the first thing he/she says is, "Honey, I did NOT cheat on you!"—*What are you thinking?*
- Your boss says, "Pop by my office at the end of the day today. Don't worry, you're not in trouble."—*How do your emotions react?*
- You walk into your toddler's room and she immediately says, "I don't have anything."—*Okay, honey, hand over the candy.*
- Your doctor calls and says, "I want to run a few tests. There's no need to be nervous."—*Yeah, right.*

In each example, the speaker had the best of intentions. However, their communications had the exact opposite effect than what they probably had hoped. Why does this happen?

In order to understand a sentence like "Don't do drugs," for example, a child has to think of what it means to do drugs. Just like you had to think of the word "rhinoceros" in order to understand my sentence, the child also has to picture himself or herself doing drugs so they know exactly what to avoid. Unfortunately, as we'll learn from the "if" chapter, when people imagine themselves taking an action, they become much more likely to take that action in real life, too.

The only people who have success avoiding all thoughts of "rhinoceros" are the people who don't try to avoid it at all. Instead, they *replace* it with a different thought. They give their brain something else to say yes to.

The takeaway is simple. Stop telling people what to "Just say NO" to, and start telling them what to "Just say YES" to.

WILL YOU EVER NEED A MORE FORCEFUL "YES"? ABSOLUTELY.

"I'm an entertainer on my way to a gig."

Usually this statement fascinates people and they start asking all kinds of questions. "What kind of entertainer are you?" "Do you do this full-time?" and "Can you show me something?" are all quite common. However, nobody had ever asked me what this man in uniform was about to ask me.

"May I see your work visa?"

It was my first time traveling internationally for a show, and this security officer wanted to know why I was trying to get into his country.

"What do you mean?" I genuinely had no idea what he was talking about.

"Basically, a work visa prevents foreigners from coming into our country and taking away jobs that our own citizens could be doing."

"Oh, I have good news, then. I'm not taking any jobs away, because there is nobody in the world who can do what I do."

He took a step back and looked at me hard. "Is that so?"

"Absolutely."

His demeanor changed, a lighthearted conversation followed, and then he stamped my passport.

Sometimes you only get one chance to make someone believe in you. I really am the only person in the world who can do my act—but it's not enough that I believe that. In that moment, I needed him to believe it, too. My gig depended on it.

It is for this reason that Rye Gutierrez put "absolutely" at the top of his list of "The Top 25 Power Words." He writes: "'Absolutely' is one of the best words in the English language. It answers questions definitely. It ends doubt. It gives confidence to you as a problem-solver. It removes worry, doubt, and apprehension." In short, it's a "yes" on steroids.

"YES PEOPLE," "NO PEOPLE," AND YOU

When people discover the power of "yes," they often quickly begin to abuse its power. "Yes" can make you popular with others. "Yes" can prevent awkward social situations. "Yes" can please the boss.

However, some people get to a point where they begin to say

yes without thinking. They say yes out of habit, and the idea of saying no for them is cringe-worthy. We often refer to these people as "yes people," "pleasers," or in extreme cases, "enablers." The rewards they get for saying yes are things like acceptance and a lack of conflict. It's the spouse who agrees with you even when they don't. It's the employee who accepts your directives even when they can't manage the workload. It's the suck-up who just wants to be your friend.

When "yes" is abused, it can result in a lack of respect, an inability to experience deep, meaningful relationships, and a loss of integrity. There's a great word for people like this:

> **milque·toast** [milk-tohst] noun (sometimes initial capital letter): a very timid, unassertive, spineless person, especially one who is easily dominated or intimidated: *a milquetoast who's afraid to ask for a raise*

Ouch.

The reverse side of this coin is what we call a "no person." This is the scrunchy-faced curmudgeon who loves telling you all the reasons why your ideas won't work. Their negativity hangs over them like a fog, blurring their perspective of the world around them. It's the impossible-to-please parent, the overly pessimistic coworker, or the change-resistant boss who is stuck in his ways despite all the evidence that proves his ways aren't working anymore.

We can't blame them. There are rewards for being a "no person" just as there are rewards for being a "yes person." First and foremost on that list of rewards is safety.

We possess an ancient survival instinct that Dr. Tom Miller says "wants to keep you the same, as you are right now, every day, for the rest of your life, until you die." The way your brain sees it—so far so good! You're breathing and your heart is beating. Let's keep that going for as long as possible. Anything new is a possible threat to that status quo. So, we say no to stuff.

This is where our fear of change comes from. This is why when anything new comes along, most people's natural gut reaction is to say no. We resist. We fear. We judge. To your brain, saying no to things, ideas, or people is almost always safer than saying yes. "No" is protection against an unknowable future.

What About You?

In a brilliant 2013 cover article for *Psychology Today*, Dr. Judith Sills suggests that we need to move our own personal "yes person/no person" lever closer to the middle ground:

> *There's a lot of talk, and a lot to be said, for the power of* Yes. Yes *supports risk-taking, courage, and an open-hearted approach to life whose grace cannot be minimized. But* No—*a metal grate that slams shut the window between one's self and the influence of others—is rarely celebrated.*

Mahatma Gandhi said it this way: "A 'no' uttered from the deepest conviction is better than a 'yes' merely uttered to please, or worse, to avoid trouble."

Sills suggests that the kind of "no" we're looking for is not the "ongoing attitude [that] expresses itself in a whining perfectionism. . . . It's a moment of clear choice."

WHEN YOU MUST SAY NO

For all the power of a "yes," there are times when you simply must say no.

When Your Integrity Is Threatened

If something is against your morals, you have to say no. When you say yes to everything in order to please other people no matter the personal cost, you end up diluting the qualities that make you *you*. The acceptance of others is simply not worth the weight of wearing a mask.

As Kurt Cobain once said, "I'd rather be hated for who I am than loved for who I am not."

When Your Plate Is Full

The biggest complaint about working with "yes people" is that they tend to get behind in their work. They agree to everything asked of them and end up being too busy to do any of it effectively. If you're committed elsewhere, say so.

When You Are Being Exploited or Abused

Cons and cheats can spot a "yes person" a mile away. If you give off that vibe, they will be attracted to you like sharks are attracted to blood in the water. In this case, the pain of having to reject another human being pales in comparison to the pain that they can cause you in the long run.

Sills advises, "If you feel you can't say no, at least to some things, some of the time, then you are not being loved—you are being controlled."

When You Have the Urge

The mark of maturity is self-discipline. Do you have the power to say no to an extra slice of cake or a cigarette, or are you a slave to your impulses?

HOW TO SAY NO

Unfortunately, "no" hurts a lot more than "yes" helps.

Human brains are all hardwired with what Dr. Roy F. Baumeister first described as a "negativity bias." This is why negative job feedback always has a more profound effect than the positive feedback you got during the very same review. This is why studies have shown that we are hurt more by losing $5,000 than we are pleased by winning $5,000. As a species, we are more compelled to avoid pain than to seek out pleasure.

Some social psychologists claim that it takes up to seven positive deposits into someone's emotional bank account to balance out just one negative withdrawal. "No" is expensive.

Knowing that there are times when "no" must be said, your job is to deliver the message and at the same time minimize the cost. Here's how.

Give Yourself Time

The key indicator of "yes people" and "no people" is that they respond to requests impulsively and habitually. Instead, give yourself time with a simple "I'll think about it." This shows that you can't be swayed by the emotions of the moment, it softens an eventual "no," and it puts you in the driver's seat.

As a parent, this was hard for me. Very quickly, my knee-jerk reaction to all of my kids' requests became "No!" Then later, when I'd thought things through, I'd change my mind to "yes." This killed the credibility of my initial "no."

The line "I'll think about it" (and the occasional "I'll have to ask your mother") was incredibly powerful in helping my "no" be "no" and my "yes" be "yes."

The "Yes Sandwich"

When a "no" must be delivered, it's helpful to be sandwiched between two "yeses." A student might ask a teacher for an extension on an assignment. Here's how the teacher might use the "yes sandwich":

"I can see that your grade is important to you. Unfortunately, I can't grant you the extension, but I can give you partial credit for the work you've done to this point."

"I can see that your grade is important to you" is beginning from a place of agreement. It counts as the first "yes." "I can't grant you the extension" is obviously the "no." "But I can give you partial credit" is the final "yes."

The formula is simple: something positive—something negative—something positive.

Intellectually, they'll get the "no" message, but it won't hurt them as much emotionally.

Give a Reason or Two Why

"Why not?" is usually the next question after I say no to my kids. When we face rejection we want to know why; it's human nature. When we give someone a reason or two why we said no to them, they can be assured that it's nothing personal and that it's not a rushed, impulsive decision. There's been some thought put into it.

Reasons that involve other people make you look less selfish for saying no. Responding to a request to help someone move with "No, I'd really rather not" is an authentic, confident refusal that can easily be perceived as selfish and downright rude. Contrast it with: "Unfortunately, I can't because my son has a huge baseball game and if I miss any of it, he'll be crushed." Now, instead of a rude jerk, you're a loving father. Perception is everything.

Change Your Language

As we've learned, "no" is quite a strong word. Try simply replacing it with euphemisms such as, "I'm going to have to decline," "I'd love to, but I can't," "I'm sorry I won't be able to commit to that," or "I'm just not comfortable moving forward with this."

Hopefully, these strategies will help you to make any necessary "no" a much easier pill for people to swallow. And as for those unnecessary "no's" . . .

THE BEST THINGS IN LIFE HAPPEN
AFTER YOU SAY "YES"

Sir Richard Branson says, "Life is a helluva lot more fun if you say yes rather than no." Google actively strives to maintain a "culture of yes" within its ranks.

Is their love for "yes" and their mega-success a coincidence? Keith Johnstone, author of *Impro*, writes: "There are people who prefer to say 'Yes,' and there are people who prefer to say 'No.' Those who say 'Yes' are rewarded by the adventures they have, and those who say 'No' are rewarded by the safety they attain." Is it possible that saying the magic word "yes" more often will actually benefit you as well as those who hear you say it? Is it possible that there is a world of opportunity and adventure out there that will never be touched by those whose automatic default setting is "no"?

As it turns out . . . yes.

Just ask my wife.

"YES" AT A GLANCE

- The word "yes," spoken to yourself as a response to a positive outcome question, has been shown to instantly increase your ability to influence those around you.
- "Yes" is magical because it communicates acceptance— which psychologists have long identified as a deep human need and critical to all relationships.
- No matter how disagreeable a person may be, there is always something you can agree on. Be willing to find that first "yes" and use it as a starting point.

- Getting a person to say a minimum of three "little yeses" early in a conversation increases the likelihood that you'll have a positive influence on the outcome of that conversation.
- Reinforce their agreeable statements by following them with "Yes and . . ."
- Avoid using disappearing negatives.
- There is some evidence to suggest that related words, like "absolutely," have a similar positive effect.
- Don't abuse the power of "yes" by becoming a "yes person." There are times when it is appropriate, even necessary, to say no.
- People who say yes are rewarded with more adventure. People who say no are rewarded with more safety.

"BUT"

While some other magic words in this book might have multiple effects on the brains of those who hear and speak them, the word "but" has only one superpower. But it's a good one. I call it . . .

THE BUT EFFECT

Human beings have long known that in any sentence, anything that comes *after* the word "but" is FAR more important than whatever comes before. That's why we mentally erase everything we hear just before the word "but" and direct our attention intently to what comes after it. Take a look at the But Effect in action:

"I'd love to go out with you, but I can't."

"It's a great idea, but I just can't invest in it right now."

"You're perfect for the position, but we had to go with someone else."

"Honey, I love you, but you've got to stop doing that."

"Great job on the project last week, but there's one area you can improve on next time."

There are two halves to the But Effect: the But Eraser and the But Enhancer. I don't care what they sound like; these are not late-night infomercial products.

For the listener, everything said *before* the word "but" is erased, and everything *after* the word "but" is enhanced. Especially if what follows the "but" is the exact opposite of what preceded the "but." Most often, this power is used recklessly, and more harm is done than good. Let's listen in on Ted and Sarah.

SARAH: You know, Ted, I just love geraniums.
TED: Yes, geraniums are nice.

So far, so good! He found the common ground and dropped in the magic word "yes" perfectly. Then . . . he makes a rookie mistake and blows it entirely.

TED: But chrysanthemums have always been my favorite.

"But . . ."?! He said, "but"?! Seriously? It's as though the magic word "yes" *never even happened*. Why do all that hard work if you're just going to ruin it two seconds later? Sarah becomes another victim of someone who doesn't know how to use the But Eraser.

Here's another example of the But Eraser in effect. You just got called into the boss's office, and you have no idea why. It's 4:30 on a Friday afternoon. As you open the door, you're invited to come in and to "please close the door behind you and have a seat."

Uh-oh.

The boss starts by regaling you with all kinds of praise. However, you can't hear any of it because you're waiting for the "but." You know it's coming. It's just a matter of when.

Suddenly, the praise stops. The body language shifts. The pause grows just a little bit too long. And then, the other shoe drops . . .

"But . . ."

BOOM! It's like a bomb went off and destroyed every piece of praise that came before it. You braced yourself for it, but it doesn't change how painful that feeling is. Now you know why she picked 4:30 on a Friday to have this conversation.

Every day, people take a perfectly good magic word and abuse its power. How can we fix this? Very simply, there are two ways. First, by placing the part that you want people to remember *after* the "but," and second, using the word "but" to erase bad feelings from people's subconscious.

Ted could have said, "Chrysanthemums have always been my favorite, but geraniums are nice." By changing only the order of the words and not the words themselves, Ted has transformed the meaning of his sentence. Not the literal meaning, of course. Those two sentences technically mean the exact same thing.

What Ted changed was the *emotional* meaning—which, of course, is everything.

If you can't change the order of the sentence, you can still eliminate the But Effect simply by removing the word "but" and replacing it with the word "and." Let's have Ted try this one.

TED: Yes, geraniums are nice *and* chrysanthemums have always been my favorite.

Once again, the literal meaning of the sentence does not change. You wouldn't want it to. There are times when the boss has to deliver bad news, or when you should be expressing a different opinion from someone else's. However, there's no need to make people feel negative emotions while you do it. It's possible to disagree agreeably.

Most people are taught to always avoid the word "but" or to always replace it with the word "and." While it is appropriate to remove the "but" in situations like the one above, there are other circumstances where "but" is the absolute best thing you can say. And they happen more often than you might think. In these cases, you'll want to bring out the intentional But Eraser.

THE INTENTIONAL BUT ERASER

Instead of erasing agreement, the But Eraser should be used to erase disagreement.

In order to understand the kinds of disagreements we're looking to erase, we first need to understand the difference between a soft "no" and a hard "no." Derek Halpern of SocialTriggers.com says, "If someone is threatening to punch you in the face, you can be sure that's a hard no. If not, then you should keep pressing to see if you can get the yes. A master persuader will always turn a soft no into a yes."

An example of a soft no is the classic "Maybe later."

Here's how you can use an intentional But Eraser to start the process of turning that into a "yes": "You could wait until later, but what if you forget? We're here and we can take care of everything right now, so later you can relax and know it's all taken care of."

The formula is simple. Start by repeating back what their disagreement was, add the word "but" to erase that thought, and follow up with what you hope for them to believe. This is much more effective than a direct response like "You really should take care of it now."

Here's another example of a soft "no" that can be overcome with the intentional But Eraser: "I'm not interested." I realize that one seems an awful lot like a hard "no" on paper. However, how it's said is important. If they're screaming it at you, then it's a hard "no." There's a chance, though, that it is simply pattern behavior—something said out of habit without even thinking about it. That's a soft "no," and you've got a great response:

"You might not be interested now, but 87 percent of our happy clients started out by saying that they weren't interested."

ADDRESSING THE UNVOICED SOFT "NO"

Sometimes you will "feel" their soft "no" before they even say it. Maybe you know the individual all too well, or maybe you've seen this situation a thousand times. Experienced communicators very often know what the soft "no" will be ahead of time. It never hurts to address these thoughts with an intentional But Eraser. Some examples:

"I know you don't like to wash the dishes, but I also know that you like doing nice things for your mom when she's stressed."

"I know it seems everyone is asking you for money this time of year, but I also know that you're one of the most committed contributors to our organization."

"I know you're against taking medication, but this is quickly becoming a matter of life and death."

"I know you're supposed to hate homework, but this assignment might actually be fun."

"I know you're busy, but you've got to see this."

INTENTIONAL BUT ERASER + "YES" = MAGIC X 2

Remember Sally from the last chapter? She used the magic word "yes" in tandem with a more subtle version of the intentional But Eraser to help Eric make the decision to join the gym. Here's how she did it—this time with my commentary in parentheses:

SALLY: What brings you in today?

ERIC: Well, I think it's about time I get in shape. *(That's a statement in alignment with the goal of joining her gym, so Sally says . . .)*

SALLY: Yes, and you've come to the right place!

ERIC: Wellll, that's what I'm trying to figure out. I've got some other options to look at still. *(Uh-oh, that's a negative statement. It's time to erase it with the But Eraser.)*

SALLY: But you're here! Obviously there's a good reason for that?

ERIC: You're the closest gym to my house. *(That's a good thing . . .)*

SALLY: Yes, and we have five hundred other locations worldwide, too. Obviously, a gym membership doesn't do you any good if you don't ever go, right?

ERIC: Yeah, I've gone down that road before. *(A negative thought. Don't worry, here comes a well-placed But Eraser . . .)*

SALLY: But somehow I get the feeling this time is totally different for you. Tell you what, let me give you a tour, and then we'll come back here and I'll show you some numbers.

ERIC: Okay, sounds good.

You can see how Sally is strengthening the positives and minimizing the negatives with each "yes, and" or "but" response. This is a very powerful technique. Once she had fostered enough agreement, she went into a call to action that featured a technique known as "and" linking.

"AND" LINKING

The word "and" is the opposite of the word "but." Instead of erasing the idea that came before it, a well-placed "and" *links* two ideas together as one.

She transitioned the dialogue with the sentence "Let me give you a tour and show you some numbers." He's very likely to agree to the tour because he's there for the sole purpose of checking out the gym. However, he might have been resistant to looking at some numbers. By putting them together, Sally made it much more likely for him to agree to both.

When you use "and" linking, be sure to put the most agreeable idea first. Then drop in an "and," followed by the suggestion that you really hope they will accept.

The next two techniques that take advantage of the But Effect were taught to me by Kenton Knepper, the creator of "Wonder Words"—a very popular program that teaches magicians how to use the power of words to improve their shows—and a master of "linguistic deception." They both take advantage of "but's" superpower very nicely.

BUT REVERSALS

What if someone uses the intentional But Eraser on you? They follow the same formula by first telling you what you want to hear, adding in a "but," and following up with what they want you to believe. Here's the most common example:

"I'd love to, but I can't."

It's very likely that someone has said this to you in one form or another at some point in your life. It's a polite way to decline someone without hurting their feelings. This particular language pattern has become just that—a pattern. It's something that comes out of our mouths without us even having to think about it.

Kenton suggests breaking that pattern with a But reversal. Your goal here isn't to change the facts. Your goal is to change the feeling.

All you're going to do is repeat back what they said to you, after making just one small adjustment.

"You can't, but you'd love to?"

You've reversed the order. Remember, "but's" superpower is to erase what comes before it and enhance what comes after it. This technique may not immediately change people's minds, but it does change the way they feel about the interaction. The focus shifts from the "I can't" part to the "I'd love to," and this affects how the conversation is remembered.

THE BUT CAUSE-AND-EFFECT FORMULA

Before we dive into Knepper's technique, it's important to understand its goal. All communication has a goal. All too often, we enter into a communication without any idea of exactly what we want the other person (or the other people) to believe, feel, or do. Knowing the answer to each one of those is important. When possible, answer each of the following questions before you begin a conversation, a pitch, or a presentation.

What Action Do You Want Them to Take?

Remember, our goal is not to get people to simply say yes to us. Our goal is to move people to action. What *specifically* is the action that you want them to take? If you're not clear about this, then they won't be either.

How Do They Need to *Feel* in Order to Take That Action?

My good friend and fellow mentalist from the UK, Kennedy, turned me on to this very important question.

Too often, people focus only on logic when trying to be influential. "If they could only see the benefits, then they would join my program!" That's not necessarily true. People make their decisions based on emotion first, and then they back them up with logic. Logic helps, but ultimately it's feelings that move people to action.

Very often, people will not have a desire to do what you want them to (such as exercise more, or clean their rooms, etc.). That's why you must focus on stirring within them the desires that they do have (a healthy body, being part of a loving family that helps each other out, etc.).

An understanding of human nature helps to pinpoint someone's true feelings and desires, and a deep knowledge of that particular person or situation helps even more. This is why people who have lived through something are always more influential in that situation than those who haven't. People who have lived it know exactly how it *feels*.

What Do They Need to *Believe* in Order for Them to Feel That Way?

Beliefs are embedded deeper in the mind than feelings. Feelings change quickly, but beliefs tend to be more constant throughout a person's life.

If you sell used cars and your prospect has the belief *Never trust a used-car salesman,* then that's a belief you'll have to overcome. If you sell information products, then before you can make a sale, you need your prospect to believe that information is valuable.

If you're having trouble getting someone to take an action, then use these three questions to help get you back on track. Nail down *exactly* what the desired action is, then reverse-engineer what someone would need to believe and how they would need to feel in order to take that action.

Once you've got all that information, pick any desired action, feeling, or belief and plug it into the "effect" portion of Knepper's "But Cause-and-Effect" formula:

[[[Cause]]], but you may [[[Effect]]].

Let me give you an example from my show. A desired effect I have is for the audience to stand at the end and applaud. A standing ovation is not just good for my ego, it also shows my client that the audience enjoyed the program. The main reason I try to earn a standing ovation, though, is that it actually increases the audience's enjoyment of the show. All things being equal, those who stand and applaud will remember having a better time than those who don't. So, "give me a standing ovation" is the desired effect.

Next you'll need to make up a cause. It can be anything. In my example, the cause of the standing ovation is "opening the envelope."

After plugging in the cause and the effect, and after making a few tweaks so everything sounds normal, I added the following line to my show. Just as I hand an envelope to a volunteer, I say tongue in cheek, "We're going to open that envelope, but they may give me a standing ovation, so we're going to save that for the end."

This line obviously wouldn't work if it was inserted into a terrible show or if there wasn't actually something amazing inside the envelope, but it has helped me to get a standing ovation at nearly every single show.

Here are some examples of this formula as it applies to everyday life:

An infomercial spokeswoman who wants to increase sales: "I'm going to show you how this works, but you may find yourself pulling out your phone to place an order."

A dentist who wants his patients to feel relaxed: "I'm going to put your chair back, but you may become so relaxed that you'll want to fall asleep."

A financial adviser to his client: "I'm going to lay out all your options, but you may want to take my advice on this one."

Depending on your personality, you may be able to pull these off in a serious tone or you may have to say them with a wink and a smile.

KICKING THE BUT HABIT

If you've been using the word "but" incorrectly then you've probably been doing so for a long time. Old habits are hard to break, but there's hope. The good news is that you don't have to worry about being perfect. You can expect to make mistakes as you develop this new skill, and that's perfectly okay. Here's the process for kicking the But habit:

Week #1: Notice how other people use the word "but." Ask yourself, *Would I have used it differently?* Replay the conversations in your mind and replace any poorly used "buts" with intentional "buts."

Week #2: Try to catch yourself saying "but" in your daily interactions. Ask yourself, *Did I use the But Effect properly in that situation? If not, how would I use it differently if I had the chance to do it over again?*

Week #3: Challenge yourself to intentionally use one But Eraser and one But Enhancer this week.

After twenty-one days of focusing on all the "buts" you hear and say, you will be amazed at how your brain has adapted to this powerful new communication technique. You will love it when But Erasers and But Enhancers are working for you instead of against you.

"BUT" AT A GLANCE

- A "but" erases what came before it and enhances what comes after it.
- This power is often accidentally misused, but when used intentionally it can have a very positive impact on the outcome of a communication.
- Intentional But Erasers can help to overcome a soft "no."
- Combine "yes" and "but" during a dialogue to create a nearly hypnotic effect.
- "And," which is the opposite of "but," can be used to eliminate the But Effect as well as link an agreeable idea to a less agreeable idea—making the less agreeable idea more likely to be accepted.

- If someone uses a But Eraser against you, no worries. You can simply repeat the statement back to them while reversing its order to improve how someone remembers the interaction.
- The powerful "But Cause-and-Effect" formula can lead people to specific actions, feelings, or beliefs.
- Breaking old speech patterns is hard. Take the three-week challenge to kick the But habit.

"BECAUSE"

Like many magicians, I got my start performing at little kids' birthday parties. Just about anything you can imagine (plus some things you can't) has happened in the middle of my show. I've had kids throw up on each other, I've had to dodge flying karate kicks *Matrix*-style, and I've even had someone's pet goat try to eat one of my props. But the most predictable of all distractions was when the kids would get overexcited and stand up in the middle of my routine. Getting the kids to remain seated was nearly impossible. That's when I stumbled upon my first real magic word.

"Because."

If I told those kids to "sit crisscross-applesauce because the kids behind you can't see," then they did. If I said, "Have a seat because I don't want all these standing ovations to go to my head," then they did. Like magic.

Only it wasn't magic. And it didn't have anything to do with the reasons I gave them, either. Instead, it was Harvard University psychologist Ellen Langer's quirky discovery in action.

Langer's famous study began when there was a line of people waiting to use a photocopier. Then she tried cutting in line. She wasn't rude about it, though. She asked politely, "Excuse me, I have five pages. May I use the Xerox machine?" Over and over she tried this and found that 60 percent of the people allowed her to go ahead of them.

Then Langer got more specific. "Excuse me, I have five pages. May I use the Xerox machine because I'm in a rush?" When she gave a reason, "because I'm in a rush," the rate of compliance shot up to 94 percent. No real surprise there.

The surprise comes with the third question: "Excuse me, I have five pages. May I use the Xerox machine, because I have to make some copies?" The rate of compliance stayed about the same, at 93 percent, even though *she removed the reason*. Langer was able to cut in line simply by using the word "because." Sounds like a magic word to me.

THE MAGIC BEHIND "BECAUSE"

When my kids were about two years old, they drove us crazy with the "Why?" game. No matter what we said, they wanted to know why. All kids go through this natural phase of brain development. This is the time when the brain's left hemisphere is coming online and the concept of cause and effect is beginning to form. This is also the time when most parents start to go a little insane.

From that point onward, our brain wants to feel like it understands the cause for every effect it observes. This is why random acts of violence and other senseless crimes bother us so much. We cry out, "Why did this have to happen?"

Notice—and this is important—the brain only wants to *feel* like it understands the cause. It doesn't actually have to understand the cause.

If you were to ask one hundred people why they can't fly, they might answer, "Because of gravity," and they'd be happy with that answer. But they don't really understand what causes gravity. I'm not sure anyone does, either. Gravity is not an explanation of the phenomenon, it's just a name for it. But that name, along with the word "because," satisfies our brains' need for causality.

This is also true for the infamous "because I said so." That's not a reason! However, parents worldwide have discovered that this phrase assures the listener's brain that there IS indeed a cause. In fact, the word "cause" is even embedded right in the word "because."

Although "because" is a magic word, it doesn't completely eliminate the need for an actual, logical reason. After all, Langer's research did show a tiny drop-off when the reason was removed. Granted, it was a negligible difference, but it was a difference nonetheless.

Here's what I've noticed: as the task increases in complexity or effort, the reason for doing it must also be increased.

This is why "because" truly has a magical effect on snap decisions with relatively little importance. If you want someone to take out the garbage, or donate a dollar to charity, or let you use the copier first, then the word "because" will be quite effective. However, for it to have influence on something more significant, like an employee's motivation level, it must be followed with a

reason that satisfies the craving for a good answer to the inces-
sant "why?" that every brain over the age of two is asking.

THE ONLY REASONS THAT MOTIVATE HUMANS

According to Abraham Maslow's famous hierarchy of needs,
there are five types of needs that all human beings strive to sat-
isfy. These five needs are the root cause for every action we take.
If you hope to motivate someone to take any kind of significant
action, then giving them a "because" followed by one of the five
needs will create a motivational maelstrom that will be difficult
for them to ignore.

Modern models have attempted to update Maslow's original
list, and some diagrams have as many as ten levels with obscure
titles and confusing explanations. While I agree that Maslow's
pyramid isn't perfect, there is some beauty in its simplicity.

Here, I'll present you with six human motivators. They are "need
to," "have to," "want to," "choose to," "love to," and "called to." I've
found the best way to explain them is by telling the following story:

*Imagine for a moment that I woke you up early and dragged you
into the city just in time for the morning rush. The air is crisp, the
sun is fresh, and you've got a large cup of hot morning fuel in one
hand. We're both a bit groggy, and so is everyone else.*

*As we chat, a sea of people forms around us—too slowly to even
notice. They're all busily heading off to work with their briefcases
in one hand and their overcoats held tightly with the other. We're
not going to have much time with any of them today, so I suppose
we should get started.*

"Excuse me, sir? Why are you going to work?"

"Um, because I got bills, man! I need to put food on the table, just like everybody else. Trust me, I'd rather be somewhere else right now if I could." He glances at his watch. If he was walking any faster, he'd be running.

He's a "need to." Does he seem motivated to you?

Absolutely. "Need to's" are motivated . . . to show up. Unfortunately, once they're there, that's all you're going to get. Have you noticed any "need to's" in your workplace? They show up, punch a clock, go through the motions, try to be as invisible as possible while they're there, take a few extra coffee breaks and/or smoking breaks, and then leave as early as possible. They're typically negative people who desperately need coffee (or perhaps some other beverage of choice) to "survive" the workweek.

Is that person truly motivated? Not really. Let's ask someone else.

"Excuse me, sir, why are you going to work?"

"I don't have a choice. I have a family. I have to put a roof over our heads. I have to pay for health insurance, and I have to make sure they're taken care of. If you'll excuse me, I have to go. I'm going to be late."

I had a feeling he'd be a "have to." "Have to's" are certainly a little more motivated than the last guy. After all, he's a provider. He's got other people to consider and care for. But once he's got his forty hours and his full-time status with benefits, he's done. No need to go above and beyond the call of duty.

There's got to be a deeper level of motivation than simply money. Let's ask another person. "Pardon me, ma'am. Why are you going to work?"

"What is this for, a survey?"

"Actually . . ."

"Oh, honey, these people may hate their jobs, but you can write on your little survey that I actually want to go to work! I like it. I like the people I work with, and it definitely beats sitting at home all day being retired! Uh-oh, I gotta take this call."

What do you think of the answer "because she wants to"? Does that mean she's motivated? A little more than the last two, that's for sure. She doesn't view work as a "necessary evil." She's probably a more positive person and definitely more fun to be around. But if you've ever known any "want to's" in the workplace, then you know that there are some downsides, too. Since they are driven by the social aspect, they might be spending too much company time socializing. They're first to keep up on all the office gossip, and they likely are spending billable hours on social media websites for personal reasons. It is 9:15, after all, and she's still standing around chatting on her cell phone.

So let's ask this woman in the pantsuit. "Why are you going to work?"

"I just got called in. I was supposed to have the day off, but there's so much going on this time of year. I'm always the first one they call, because they know I'll say yes. This kind of thing looks really good come review time."

I'm going to call her a "choose to." She's more motivated than anyone else we've talked with so far. In fact, she has crossed over the line between "doing the bare minimum" and "going above and beyond the call of duty." This is a person who wants to climb the corporate ladder and achieve success in her field. However, her motivation is often self-seeking. It's tough for this person to be a member of a team—she may even sabotage other players for her own personal gain. Also, she probably struggles to find that all-important work/life balance. Being a team player is increasingly important in today's workplace. Ultimately, if we are going to serve the company and its customers, then we need all team members to be on board for the right reasons. The biggest problem with her is that she is most interested in serving herself.

Unfortunately, I expected this. These are the most common answers you'll get when you ask people, "Why are you going to work?" The sad truth is, the majority of Americans hate their jobs.

The remaining levels of motivation are called "love to" and "called to."

A "love to" person has a hard time telling the difference between business and pleasure. They don't think of what they do as "work," because they love it so much.

A person who feels "called to" their work has motivation that goes even deeper. This person says, "I do what I do because there is a customer I serve, there is a cause I support, or there is a purpose I have that's bigger than just myself."

This person is incredibly motivated and thoroughly fulfilled in their work, and it just doesn't get any better than this. Volunteer organizations show us that when you tap into this level of motivation, it's not about money anymore. By definition, volunteers are not paid, and yet they show up and give their all anyway.

"Love to's" and "called to's" are not just motivated by survival like the "need to's" and the "have to's" are. They're not just motivated by punishments and rewards like the "want to's" and the "choose to's" are. Their motivation is intrinsic. It comes from within.

If your hope is to motivate or inspire those around you, then you need to start by helping them to find a "because" that their brains can feel good about.

So, which "because" will work best? Here's a tip: don't bother asking them outright, "What will motivate you?" They'll probably answer, "More money!"

The science has shown that money doesn't motivate people, just as money doesn't make people happy. However, it is still tempting for employees to believe that it will. I once saw a sign in a shop window that illustrates this deception perfectly. It read: "All I ask is the chance to prove that money can't make me happy."

A more productive question to ask would be: "Why did you choose this career path?" or "Why did you choose this company?" In their answers you'll find what really drives them. Once you have that, all you'll have to do is remind them by using the techniques in this chapter.

"BECAUSE" WILL NEVER WORK WITHOUT THIS FOUNDATION

You can't encourage others to be motivated by the levels of "love to" or "called to" unless you are motivated by them yourself.

Great leaders and motivators have a passion for what they do that goes beyond earning a living. This passion is contagious to those around them.

My grandfather was one of only two people in my life who encouraged me in my pursuit of a career in magic. While everyone else was telling me to focus on finding something more realistic and hoping that I would outgrow the phase, he urged me to keep practicing. His pure joy at watching my magic inspired me like nothing else. Every time I saw him he'd ask, "Any new tricks?" or "Got any gigs coming up?"

I didn't know this at the time, but long before I was even born he dabbled as an amateur magician. I discovered this shortly after showing him my first fumbling card trick. He smiled as he watched patiently. When I was finished, he quietly held his hand out for the cards and proceeded to blow my ten-year-old mind with incredible sleight-of-hand tricks. I was hooked.

He never pursued magic as a career. Instead, he ended up working as a janitor until he was in his eighties.

Here's the thing: he *loved* his job. While other people looked down on his profession, he changed his perspective. He didn't expect his job to bring meaning to his life; he brought meaning to his job. Never once did I hear him complain about work. In fact, whenever I went to the clinic where he worked, the staff treated me like royalty, because I was "Eddie's grandkid." He was always upbeat and positive at work.

It wasn't his position I respected. It wasn't just the fact that he was my grandfather. It certainly wasn't his money, his physical strength, or his tiny apartment.

It was his perspective. He didn't motivate me just by telling me a "because." He showed me.

If you don't have your own compelling "because," then it will be very hard for you to give one to others. So let me ask you, "Why are *you* going to work?"

It's pretty tough to convince anyone to love their work or to pursue their calling if you're stuck in the humdrum, day-to-day, "need to" stage yourself. If this is you, then it looks like you've got a choice to make. You can either change your perspective, or you can change your profession. That's it. In this land of opportunity and in this time of abundance, there's really no excuse for a job that makes you miserable. We spend far too much of our lives at work for it to be anything less than fulfilling. So again, either do what you love or love what you do.

However, don't rush to quit your job! Don't head to your boss's office screaming and yelling about how "magic boy" told you that you need to change your profession in order to be happy. Changing your profession should be a last resort. The grass is not always greener on the other side of the fence. The grass is greener where it's watered.

Now that you have the basics of a good "because," let's take a look at some advanced techniques.

THE SQUARE SUGGESTION SECRET AND ABT

People don't believe what you tell them. They rarely believe what you show them. They often believe what their friends tell them. They always believe what they tell themselves.

—Seth Godin

Mentalists don't use their hands to manipulate magicians' props like ropes, coins, cards, or scarves. Instead, they use their words to manipulate the thoughts, beliefs, and perceptions of an audience.

Let me show you an example of a simple trick that can be done with words. Read and follow these instructions:

Right now, I want you to think of a simple geometric shape, such as a square or a . . . whatever. Got one? Great. Now think of another one. You should now be thinking of two simple geometric shapes.

If you're like most people, you thought of a circle and a triangle.

Did I predict the future? Of course not, but the secrets behind this little illusion are quite revealing. The first part of the secret points to the brain's love of shortcuts. The brain doesn't want to work any harder than it has to. Circle and triangle come to mind first because they are the simplest answers. So, by using the words "right now," the mentalist creates a sense of urgency, almost rushing your choice. This gives you a perceived time limit, which makes your brain want to rely on shortcuts even more.

The word "simple" is a relative term that eliminates a slew of possible choices. Obviously, choices like "triskaidecagon," "enneagon," and "icosagon" are out. But even questionable choices like "rhombus," "pentagon," and "octagon" aren't commonly chosen either. When you're on stage in front of two hundred people, you don't want to be the idiot who doesn't follow directions well.

Quite important to this process is the phrase "such as a square." By suggesting "square," the mentalist virtually eliminates the possibility that you will choose a square. One of the most predictable things about people is that we don't believe we are predictable. This little illusion takes full advantage of that. "Square" is the mentalist's idea, not your idea. So you reject it and think of "your own" idea, which, of course, is what he wanted you to think all along.

Here's the main point: in order to influence someone to your way of thinking, they must first believe that it is their own way of thinking. True influence is not about persuading, manipulating, or cajoling people. Rather, it is about leading them.

How do you feel when someone is giving you the hard sell or pressuring you into something? What about when your manager is bossing you around? You probably don't feel like "going with the flow." When pushed, we humans tend to put up our defenses and resist.

When such resistance is present, "because" loses some of its magic. Even if you were to add a very compelling reason, there just comes a point when the other person is going to reject it no matter what you say. If they appear impervious to the power of the magic word "because" for any reason, then it's time to up the ante and try some ABT (Advanced Because Technique).

The idea behind ABT is to get the person to say "because" to themselves. Instead of giving someone a thousand reasons to do something, try asking them, "Why?" When you do that, they will fill in their own "because." Now it's their reasons, not yours. Therefore, those reasons will hold more sway in their future decisions and behavior. In a way, "why" is almost a magic word of its own, because it indirectly taps into the power of "because."

A Rotary Club president might ask her members, "Why do you suppose we have an attendance requirement in this organization?" in order to increase attendance. A car salesperson may ask the customer, "Why are you looking at a Hyundai today?" in order to increase the likelihood of getting the sale. Parents might ask their children, "Why is it important to treat other people with respect?" in order to encourage kind behavior. A doctor may ask his patient, "Why should you be exercising more?" in order to increase patient compliance.

Asking "why?" in these ways forces the listener to actively engage in any "because" reasons that follow. People are always more likely to take an action if they think it is their idea. We tend to diminish other people's ideas and inflate our own.

So, I'll follow my own advice. Why do you think it's sometimes better to ask "why?" than to tell people "because"?

THE TRAILING "OR . . ."

Here's another great ABT. This is particularly useful if someone responds to your "why?" with a shrug and an "I don't know."

You'll start by offering one or more obvious "because" reasons. Then you'll end with a trailing "or . . ." statement. Here's an example:

"Some people get into this line of work just for the money, or the recognition, or the benefits. And others are here for the people that we serve, or the difference that we make, or . . . any number of reasons."

The magic happens during the long pause between the words "or" and "any."

The human brain tends to operate in survival mode, meaning it is always anticipating what is about to happen next. One of the things that separates us from the rest of the animal kingdom is something called "Theory of Mind." This describes the distinctly human ability to interpret and anticipate other people's thoughts, beliefs, or intentions.

During the pause after the word "or," the listener's mind can't help but immediately start filling in the blank space. Think about what you've just accomplished. Their brains are creating and exploring their own "because" reasons! Or, at the very least, they're trying to anticipate what your next suggestion might be.

There is something else you must know about the trailing "or." Don't expect people to make a huge leap from your suggestions to their own answers. How their mind fills in the blank will depend on the suggestions that you provide immediately before the trailing "or." For example, if you were to use this technique to ask someone to "think of any number like 8, or 17, or 4, or . . . any number at all," they probably won't make the jump to 59,835. Of course, it's possible they will. But in my experience, this almost never happens.

Did you notice the trailing "or" in the circle/triangle trick? The suggestion "square" right before the trailing "or" primed your mind to think of a *really* simple shape. If I had said "hexagon" instead of "square," then your answers would likely be closer to "octagon" and "pentagon" rather than "circle" and "triangle."

This is a great technique that can help you be a better parent, salesperson, leader, motivator, or . . . in just about any area of life!

"BECAUSE" CAN HELP YOU LEAD—THE CLARITY TEST

An essential piece of your job is getting the entire team on board with the organization's goals and vision. Without "buy-in," your staff will lack motivation and enthusiasm, and their overall performance will suffer in a big way. You absolutely *must* provide them with a crystal-clear vision.

In short, you need a "because."

Don't ever assume they know what the organization's vision is. Don't even assume that *you* know. Here's a test you can do right now to determine how clear your vision is: grab a pen and write out the answers to the three questions below. Set a timer for two minutes and start writing. You should be able to clearly write one or two sentences for each question below before time runs out.

What is your organization's mission?

_____

_____

_____

_____

_____

What is your department's mission?

_____

_____

_____

_____

_____

What is your mission as team leader?

_____

_____

_____

_____

_____

Don't skip this exercise. I don't care if you never refer back to this page; I still want you to write out your answers anyway. Consider this: if you can't write down concise answers to the above questions in two minutes or less, then your vision isn't clear enough in your mind. If it's not clear in your mind, then how can you ever expect it to be clear in the minds of your direct reports? Test yourself now. Can you physically write them out on paper? (Just thinking the answers in your head doesn't count. A new kind of clarity emerges when you actually put those thoughts on paper. Try it and see.)

Next, try testing your staff. If you were to ask them, "Quick, what's our vision?" would they be able to answer you in one quick sentence in thirty seconds or less? If you asked multiple team members, would you get the same exact answers? If not, then your team could use a little more clarity of vision.

"BECAUSE" CAN HELP YOU SELL

People don't buy what you do. They buy why you do it. The goal is not to do business with everybody who needs what you have. The goal is to do business with people who believe what you believe.

—Simon Sinek, author of _Start with Why_

Sinek builds the case that when successful mega-brands like Apple communicate with the marketplace, they always begin by providing a "because." Instead of telling you why you need to do business with them, they tell you why they're in business.

Apple customers are fiercely loyal because they share Apple's "because." They find the traits of challenging the norm and thinking differently within themselves (or they hope to), and then they buy Apple products as a means of personal expression. They're not buying because of a list of features and benefits. They're buying to support a "because" that they can feel good about. In doing so, they feel a sense of connection, belonging, and even community.

Things like purpose, mission, and a sense of social belonging will always drive people to action more than a list of features and benefits will. This is true because of the physiology of the human brain.

The brain's neocortex is the seat of language, conscious thought, and logic. This is the part of the brain that most sales pitches are targeted at. However, the brain's limbic system is responsible for emotional responses, behaviors, and all decision making. How do you target that? Simple—tell everyone your "because" and people who share the same "because" will flock to you, they'll trust you, and they'll buy from you.

You can earn business success by being the best, the fastest, or the cheapest, and you'll always run the risk of being knocked off the top of the hill by someone else. Or, you can earn business success by finding and leading a group of people who share your "because," and you'll never want for anything for the rest of your life.

"BECAUSE" AT A GLANCE

- ▪ "Because" is magical because it satisfies the brain's need for a link between cause and effect.

- ▪ "Because" doesn't always need a logical or compelling reason behind it in order to be effective, unless you want to motivate someone to complete significant or complex tasks.

- ▪ The six most compelling reasons are: "need to," "have to," "want to," "choose to," "love to," and "called to."

- ▪ Reasons are less compelling to others if you don't believe them yourself.

- ▪ When resistance is present, try ABT (Advanced Because Technique).

- ▪ Leaders—make sure your team members understand the organization's "because" in addition to their own "because."

- ▪ Salespeople—people don't buy what you do, they buy why you do it. Freely broadcast your own "because" to the world, and start attracting loyal customers and clients who share it.

THEIR NAME

One of the richest men in America was burning my hands.

That's magician lingo. It means I couldn't shake the multibillionaire's gaze away from the secret move that I needed to do. He was dialed in. If I tried anything sneaky now, I was busted. I cracked a halfhearted joke.

Nothing.

Fortunately, I caught a break. Someone behind him called out his name. "Excuse me, Mr. Redstone!"

It worked. It broke the spell. He snapped out of it for a brief moment and I grabbed my chance. The years of practice paid off, and I executed the move swiftly—knowing that he wouldn't notice anything had changed when he regained his focus. (This is a phenomenon known as "change blindness." We magicians take advantage of that particular observational flaw all the time.) The rest of my routine went off without a hitch. Laughter, applause, and I was off to the next table.

In the case of my experience with Mr. Redstone, the impact of hearing his name was obvious. But why did this happen? More important, how can you strategically use the power of names with coworkers, employees, and bosses?

LISTENING LEVELS

It all starts with how your brain processes sound information. As long as your ears work, you hear everything around you. *Everything.* It's your brain's job to tune out the unimportant and focus on the important. It can literally turn sounds on and off like a switch (which is helpful if you're married). We call this process "paying attention."

According to Brown University auditory neuroscientist Seth S. Horowitz, there are three different levels of listening attention:

"Top-down" is what we traditionally think of when it comes to paying attention. This is when you are actively engaged in listening to something or someone. This is surprisingly difficult to do! In fact, it's amazing that it ever happens at all. With all the distractions and media and technology vying for our attention, it's no wonder that listening is a dying art. More on this later.

Then there's the "bottom-up" response, which, in brain nerd jargon, is called the "stimulus-directed response." This happens when you hear a sound that is out of place ("Is that a banjo?") or when you hear your name called out in a crowded shopping center. Your brain gives this kind of sound priority attention over the top-down pathway. You could be in mid-conversation (or trying to figure out a magic trick), but hearing your name will fire off your bottom-up response and "magically" commandeer your attention.

Sudden loud noises are more important to your survival than any other sound, and your brain gives them top priority. The chain of neurons between your ears and your spine is only five neurons long, and it only takes about a tenth of a second for your body to start reacting to a sudden loud noise. It takes more than half a second for your brain to start forming the framework for cognition. That explains why you jump before you consciously realize that you've heard something. You've probably had this experience if you've ever watched a horror movie—despite your best efforts to control it. We may find a way to take advantage of this third level, the "startle response," later on. For now, let's stick with names.

THE SWEETEST SOUND

With their brilliantly titled paper "Why Susie Sells Seashells by the Seashore: Implicit Egotism and Major Life Decisions," Brett W. Pelham, Matthew C. Mirenberg, and John T. Jones out of State University of New York at Buffalo suggest that "there may be much more in a name than most people realize."

They were able to show an astonishing connection between people's names and the decisions they make. Get this: if your name is Cathy, you're more likely to crave Coke, but if your name is Peter, then you probably prefer Pepsi—statistically speaking, of course.

This "Name-Letter Effect" is nothing new, and it has already been shown to influence minor decisions in people from at least fourteen different countries. What makes this paper special is that the authors were able to show that we actually allow the letters in our names to influence our major life decisions as well, such as where to buy a home or what kind of career to pursue.

For example, they found that if your name is Denise, you are more likely to become a dentist and less likely to become a lawyer—simply because "Denise" shares more letters with "dentist" than with "lawyer." It's also why Harry runs a hardware store while Rodney does roofing. It may even explain why I live in Taunton and (t)each (i)nfluence and (m)otivation.

It's tempting to explain this away as mere coincidence, but this effect is surprisingly prevalent. Among their impressive list of findings is the fact that the state of Virginia boasts 30 percent more residents named Virginia than statistics should indicate, Louisiana's got 47 percent more guys named Louis than it should, and there are a whopping 88 percent more people named Georgia living in the state of Georgia than would be predicted by relative proportions.

Despite how hard it is to believe that our choices may be influenced by anything other than our own free will, there's no denying that the Name-Letter Effect is very real. According to Pelham, et al.: "Because most people possess positive associations about themselves, most people prefer things that are connected to the self (e.g., the letters in one's name)."

Dale Carnegie intuited this in his classic book *How to Win Friends and Influence People* when he penned: "Remember that a person's name is, to that person, the sweetest and most important sound in any language."

As it turns out, a name is more magical than even he thought. Let's learn how to put some of that magic to good use.

USING NAMES WISELY—PART 1:
WHEN YOU WANT BUY-IN

This is an especially important technique for managers and leaders in order to make their team feel prized. People don't leave their jobs because they don't make enough money. More often, people quit their jobs because they feel underappreciated. Make sure each member of your team feels valued and important. Notice I did not say, "*Tell* each member of your team that they are valued and important." Instead, I said, Make sure they *feel* valued and important. They need to know that you see them as an individual person and not just a number. Turnover is too expensive to mess this up.

When people have more input into what goes on in their workplace, they tend to report higher job satisfaction than when they don't have a say in the matter. Simple, right?

What's not so simple is when you have members on your team who are introverts. By their very nature, introverts don't like to share their feelings or opinions much. Ever try throwing questions out to the room during a meeting? If you've got a room full of introverts, then the room will be silent while everyone waits for everyone else to talk. If there are one or two extroverts, then they will take over while the introverts silently mumble and complain to themselves. If this keeps happening, then the introverts may feel that their presence on the team is not all that important.

This means you've got to be proactive about always striving for consensus decision-making. In order to make everyone feel important, you've got to value everyone's opinion equally, even if they're not up front about sharing it. It's not always easy, but consensus decision-making makes for much stronger teams with higher levels of employee engagement. Remember, everyone needs to *feel* equally as important and valued as the rest of the team. To do that, you're going to have to get input from your introverts, and this seems about as easy as squeezing water out of a rock. Fortunately, I have some tips for you.

First, call on your introverts by name. Simply inviting their feedback directly often will do the trick. However, if all you get is a shrug, then it might be time to meet with the introvert one-on-one to discuss how he or she felt about the last meeting. If all you get during the meeting is a shrug and a few unintelligible mumbles, then try inviting him or her to send you an email. It's typically more comfortable for introverts to share their thoughts in writing rather than in person. (If you *still* don't get a response after all that, then it's time to try the magic word "if"—which will be featured in an upcoming chapter.)

At the very least, even if you get absolutely zero input from a team member, the very fact that you made every effort to reach out to them specifically (and by name) shows a leadership style that is committed to consensus decision-making. It shows that you value everyone, and that goes a very long way.

USING NAMES WISELY—PART 2: WHEN THEIR EMOTIONS TAKE OVER

Another time it is helpful to use someone's name is for a little psychological technique called "pattern interrupt."

Imagine you invite a team member into your office for a one-on-one. Let's also imagine that the purpose of this meeting is to inform him that his performance isn't where it needs to be. Not an easy thing for him to hear. You probably don't have to imagine what happens in this situation when his emotions take over, because you can probably remember an experience from your own life when someone "exploded" on you.

> **GEORGE:** This is bull__! After everything I've done for this company? This place is so negative. Nobody ever appreciates what I *do* around here! Everyone always—
> (*Time for a pattern interrupt.*)
> **YOU:** George! Of course we appreciate you. Obviously, there's been some kind of misunderstanding. Tell you what, let's take five minutes. Let me grab a refill of my water and we'll try this again.

George's emotions were beginning to erupt. When this happens, he tends to say and do things that he regrets later. Your job is to bring him back to his senses immediately with a pattern interrupt. He'll thank you for helping him to avoid an awkward situation.

Here's why the above script works so well: first, you used his name. Have you ever heard your name called out in a crowded place? It immediately grabs your attention, doesn't it? Anytime we hear our name, it gets us focused like nothing else. Our name speaks directly to that deeply conditioned part of our brains that makes us stop, look, and focus on whoever said it—even if just for a moment. This is our brain's "bottom-up" stimulus-directed response in action. Second, you're not only saying George's name, you're upping the ante a little bit. You're almost shouting it. This engages his startle response, which, if you'll remember, gets top priority in his brain. Be very careful when shouting at someone. You don't want to give the wrong impression and start a shouting match. Stay safe by having open body language. Hold your hands out to the side and show both of your palms. You are supposed to be assertive in this situation, not aggressive. Aggression is what happens when you allow your emotions to take over. Assertiveness is having the confidence to say how you feel. It's respecting your rights while also respecting the rights of others.

So don't be afraid to be firm. You've got to make sure you're heard. Your voice cannot be drowned out by George's rant. Remember, this is a pattern interrupt. Don't worry about interrupting George and stepping on his toes a little bit. In fact, that's kind of the whole idea. Just make sure it's done in love and you'll be fine. In addition to shouting, a visual disturbance is helpful to buy you some extra time and attention for what you've got to say next. Simply waving your hands slowly back and forth seems to do the trick.

Now that you've used the magic word to grab George's attention, let's get your money's worth. Choose your next words (and your nonverbals) carefully. Go right for the heart of the issue and reassure George's emotions with something like: "Of course we appreciate you!" Make sure to be truthful here. Even if you don't appreciate George, there's always something you can say that *is* true, such as: "Obviously there's been some kind of misunderstanding" or, "Clearly I'm not communicating as effectively as I'd like to." This is what we call beginning from a place of agreement, and it is essential if you want to avoid the dangerous dance that you and George were on the verge of locking into. (Note: see the chapter on "Yes" for more ways to quickly get people into an agreeable state.)

After the primary emotion is addressed, let's pull back on the throttle a little bit. Tone down the volume as a means of modeling the behavior that you want to see in George. This is a powerful technique that takes advantage of a fairly recent discovery in neuroscience: mirror neurons. Mirror neurons are believed to be at least partly responsible for the monkey-see-monkey-do behavior in humans. When you see someone yawn, *you're* likely to yawn. If you see me bite into a lemon, then *your* mouth will water. If you watch a horror movie and someone is covered in spiders, you will feel them crawling on *your* neck. We are incredibly social creatures, and the brain does an amazing job of making us feel connected to one another. So when you pull back on your intensity level, George is much more likely to do the same on his, because of this emotional contagion feature of the human brain.

Finally, suggest a short break while allowing George to save face. "Tell you what, let's take five minutes. Let me grab a refill of my water and we'll try this again." The break is actually more than a suggestion. It's happening, and George is not going to drag you back into the discussion until you've both had time to clear your heads. So, say the line "Tell you what, let's take five minutes" with a calm demeanor (modeling behavior). Then physically get up and start preparing for a break (as though the break has already started) while saying the line "Let me grab a refill of my water and we'll try this again." Now George can't come back with something like "I don't need a break," because the break has already started and it's for *you*, not him! Also, notice the use of words like "let's" and "we." These plural pronouns allow George to save face, because you're not pointing the finger and accusing him of anything. Instead, it's a situation that you're both in together.

HERE ARE THE STEPS:

1. Use magic word #4 (their name) loudly and with hand motions.
2. Reassure the core emotional issue ("We *do* appreciate you!").
3. Throttle back the intensity and model the behavior you want.
4. Take a break.
5. Allow George to save face.

Sounds much better than "George, calm down! You're overreacting," doesn't it? Try it and see the power of magic words in action.

That script works best when someone is showing a sudden and uncharacteristic burst of emotion. But what happens when it's not uncharacteristic? What happens when anger and yelling are someone's default setting? What do you do with those people who tend to get their own way by plowing over everyone in their path, who don't let anyone else get a word in edgewise, and who never apologize for doing it?

After you interrupt the pattern by using their name, you'll use a slightly different approach. Here's the situation: your boss walks into your office and comes at you out of nowhere. . . .

MIKE (YOUR BOSS): I just heard about what you did to George. He doesn't deserve this kind of treatment.

YOU: I understand how you—

MIKE: No, you don't understand. You never understand. You walk around here like you own the place. If it weren't for George, you wouldn't even have this position.

YOU: If I came across that way, I certainly—

MIKE: I'll tell you another thing: if anything happens to George . . . you're done. I'll make your life a living hell. You won't last a week in this organization when I turn my sights on you, you understand?

(Okay, time for a pattern interrupt.)

YOU: Mike! You're right. I handled this situation poorly. I'm already working on x, y, and z to make it right. Thanks for getting George's back on this.

Let's break down what just happened. You started with your normal, cordial approach. Then you realized that's not what Mike needed from you. Mike is a get-down-to-business kind of guy, he's assertive (more like aggressive), and he prefers to communicate with other assertive people who get to the point quickly. As soon as you see the Mikes of this world enter into this kind of pattern, it's time for an interrupt.

First things first, raise your assertiveness level to match Mike's. This does *not* mean trying to shout over him like you did with George. That will only buy you a shouting match, and Mike . . . will . . . win. Instead, simply hold your ground. Maintain eye contact and an open body posture. Listen attentively without becoming emotionally involved. Whatever you do, don't back down. Notice when Mike starts interrupting you, you turn the tables right back onto him. Use the same attention-grabbing steps you used with George. Say Mike's name (loudly, matching his intensity but not exceeding it), and use a visual disturbance such as waving your hands (while showing your open palms).

Then you say the most unexpected thing possible. (Remember,

this is designed to interrupt a pattern. It has got to be strikingly *different*.) "You're right! I handled this situation poorly." (Or whatever they're accusing you of.) This will absolutely stop Mike in his tracks. Now you can start backing off on the intensity. You've let him know that his point has been heard, and you've certainly gotten his attention. Once Mike knows he's been heard, his next step is to make sure that something is being done about it. So tell him.

"I'm already working on x, y, and z to make it right."

This person doesn't need apologies from you. They don't need excuses, or even explanations. What they want is progress toward results, now.

Finally, give Mike a chance to save face. "Thanks for getting George's back on this." The Mikes of the world have an incredible need to be right. If you don't make them feel as though they "won" the argument, they'll keep coming at you until they *do* feel like they've won. If you get into the ring with them, your long-term relationship will suffer. Bite the bullet, take one for the team, and make them *feel* as though they've won. Notice I did not say to lie down and take it. If you follow the steps outlined below, you will earn their respect. It's the best way to salvage a bad situation.

1. Hold your ground. Don't tolerate their interruptions.
2. Use magic word #4 (their name) while matching their intensity and waving your hands.
3. Say, "You're right," and repeat back exactly what they're accusing you of.
4. Quickly get to the bottom line. What is going to be done about it?
5. Allow Mike to save face.

NEVER FORGET A NAME AGAIN

For all the value that using someone's name brings to the table, you can really blow it big time by forgetting their name. Talk about making them feel as though they are not a valued and important person! Obviously, this cannot happen.

For those of you who have very large teams, or very high turnover, or multiple shifts that you manage, or any other reason that would make it hard for you to remember all of your team members' names, I bring good news. It's possible. Actually, it's easier than you think. Your brain is a pretty incredible thing. It is said that Charles M. Schwab could remember all the names of his more than eight thousand employees. Now, I don't know exactly how he did it, but I'm willing to bet that the following ideas excerpted from my e-book *Memory Improvement Tips* will help you do it, too.

Pay Attention

The mind is overwhelmed with stimulus when you first meet a person. Your brain is extremely busy summing up nonverbal signals to "get a vibe" from this person and make determinations about how you are going to react toward them. It takes seven seconds to form a first impression about someone. That's a lot of information for your brain to crunch in such a short period of time. It's no wonder you've already forgotten their name a minute later!

The truth is, you didn't forget it. You just never focused on it to properly hear it in the first place. Try getting into the habit of forcing yourself to listen to a person's name when you meet them. A good strategy is to condition your mind to always be thinking, *I wonder what his name is*, whenever you see someone you don't know. This generates curiosity and interest within your mind, and it helps you to be fully engaged when you hear the name.

Repeat, Repeat, Repeat!

When you hear the name, say it back to them to make sure you've got it right. For example:

STEVE: Hi, I'm Steve.
YOU: Steve? Hi, Steve, I'm _____.

You've got a better chance to remember it if you hear it once AND say it twice. In addition, you may find that you get the name wrong every once in a while. It's much better to find this out sooner rather than later. "Oh, your name is Chris! I'm so sorry that I've been calling you Rick for the last three years!"

Spell Check

Don't be afraid to ask for the spelling of unusual names. It will allow you to visualize the name better, which will help you remember. You may think you don't have to bother with the spelling for a simple name like "Matt," but what if it's "Mat" with one "t"?

20 Questions

If it doesn't make sense to ask about the spelling, how about asking a related question, such as "Is that short for Matthew?"

Anything you can think of to ask about the name is good, because it forces the brain to be engaged and creates a clearer memory.

Comment

Can't think of any questions to ask? Simply make a comment about the name. "Oh, my cousin's name is Beth." This forces you to cross-reference that name through your mental database and form a link to someone you already *do* know.

Take Advantage of Coincidence

If her name is Joan and she's an artist, then just remember "Joan of Art." If she owns a bar and her name is "Margarita," it's a perfect opportunity for this technique. This doesn't always happen, of course, but when it does, be sure to take advantage.

Once I was at a photo shoot and the photographer was named David Kammerman. Sounds an awful lot like "cameraman," doesn't it? I even used the 20 Questions method mentioned previously . . . "So I just have to ask, is that your real name?" (Yes, it was.) "Does a name like that benefit your business?" (Yes, it does.)

Funny Nicknames

If you meet a man who is very skinny and he introduces himself as Jim, then you can remember him as "Slim Jim." If his name is Tony, then you can remember him as "Bony Tony."

This shouldn't be too hard for many of us. We've been coming up with offensive nicknames for people since grade school.

Truth be told, they don't have to be offensive. It could be

"Manly Stanley" or "Awesome Al." Just make sure it is obvious and memorable.

Use It or Lose It

Get in the habit of using people's names throughout the course of your conversations. There are plenty of opportunities to do this. For example, whenever I call a company for customer service and they answer, "I'm Adam, how may I assist you?" I make it a point to use Adam's name throughout our call. Same goes for a waitress at a restaurant, a potential customer, or a new acquaintance.

You don't want to overdo this, of course ("Well, Adam, I'm glad you asked, Adam. I'll try to explain the situation to you, Adam."). But dropping in someone's name throughout a conversation is perfectly acceptable, and it creates a positive impression.

Write It Down

Obviously, taking notes is cheating. Or is it? Even if you never refer back to the note, just the physical act of writing down a name will further cement it in your memory.

If you are creating a file to refer back to, make sure you include other details besides just their name, such as where you met, what you talked about, etc.

Review

At the end of each day, ask yourself who you met during the course of the day. Review their names to help plant the memory deep inside your brain.

Photographic Name Memory

The brain has a tough time remembering names. It has a much easier time with pictures. That's why you can almost always remember a face, but the name often escapes you.

The solution is to convert a name into a mental picture (a name-picture). Once you have a name-picture, all you have to do is associate that name-picture with one of the person's most outstanding features. Maybe they have a big nose, bushy eyebrows (like me), or stunning eyes.

Let's say I've met someone named Mike, and his most noticeable feature is his big ears. My name-picture for Mike is a microphone. So I'm going to imagine that one of Mike's ears has a tiny mouth inside it and it is singing karaoke into a microphone. Now there's an unforgettable image! When you see those ears again, you can't help but have that microphone image pop into your mind. Once you see the image, you can easily convert the name-picture "microphone" back into Mike.

Maybe Shirley has a unique-looking nose. My name-picture for Shirley is a Shirley Temple drink. I would therefore imagine Shirley sneezing and a glass full of a Shirley Temple flying out of her nose.

The images are easier to remember if they are action-packed, wacky, or emotionally charged. If you try to remember Heather's name and her outstanding feature is that she has "man hands," don't imagine her picking up a feather with her hands. There's nothing special about that. People pick things up every single day. The brain will file that in the "boring" category and it will not bother to remember it. Instead, picture her "man hands" as so manly that they are growing hair out of the knuckles. Not just any kind of hair, though . . . feathers! Disturbing? Yes. Memorable? Absolutely.

This is probably the single best method for remembering names. The challenge, however, is creating a database of name-pictures in your mind. Fear not, I have some tips for you!

Start by creating ten name-pictures a day. Think of everyone you know and create a name-picture for each of their names. After two weeks of this, you'll have almost 150 name-pictures to use. *Do not* skip this step. Without a good-sized database of name-pictures, this technique will be frustrating for you.

Here is a list of name-pictures I've created for the fifty most common names in America to get you started. I'll start with the twenty-five most common male names, and then I'll give you the twenty-five most common female names. Keep in mind, the name-pictures I've made up here may or may not work for you. Some of them are natural associations for me based on my own life experiences.

Male Name-Pictures

JAMES (Jim)—a Slim Jim

JOHN—a toilet (my apologies to anyone named John)

ROBERT (Bob)—a buoy bobbing on the water's surface

MICHAEL (Mike)—a microphone

WILLIAM (Bill)—a dollar bill

DAVID—a statue

RICHARD—I'm sure you can think of something for this one

CHARLES—a river (I'm from Boston)

JOSEPH (Joe)—a cup of coffee

THOMAS (Tom)—a drum

CHRISTOPHER (Chris)—an "X" (like a crisscross)

DANIEL (Dan)—a lion (lion's den)

PAUL—a bouncing ball

MARK—a bruise (as in, "That's gonna leave a mark!")

DONALD—a duck

GEORGE—a gorge

KENNETH (Ken)—a hen

STEVEN (Steve)—a stove

EDWARD (Ed)—a bed

BRIAN—a brain

RONALD (Ron)—a man running

ANTHONY (Tony)—a skeleton (Bony Tony)

KEVIN—the number seven

JASON—a man being chased (chasin')

MATTHEW (Matt)—a welcome mat

Female Name-Pictures

MARY—the Virgin Mary

PATRICIA (Pat)—a baseball bat

LINDA—beauty crown (*linda* means "pretty" in Spanish)

BARBARA—barbed-wire fence

ELIZABETH—an ax (Lizzie Borden)

JENNIFER—a heart (Jennifer Love Hewitt)

MARIA—a wedding dress (as in, "I'm gonna marry ya")

SUSAN—a pair of socks (Susan sounds like "shoes and . . .")

MARGARET (Peg)—a pirate's peg leg

DOROTHY (Dot)—Dots candy

LISA—the *Mona Lisa*

NANCY—pants

KAREN—a carrot

BETTY—a poker chip

HELEN—a demon
SANDRA (Sandy)—the beach
DONNA—a duck (as in, Donald)
CAROL—bells ("Carol of the Bells")
RUTH—a roof
SHARON—a toddler throwing a fit because she doesn't
    want to share
MICHELLE—a missile
LAURA—an "aura"
SARAH—cheerleader's pom-poms (rah-rah!)
KIMBERLY—a very burly woman named Kim
DEBORAH—a bra

A great way to practice this technique is to jump on Facebook and just start browsing profiles. You'll have an endless supply of names and faces from which to try creating name-pictures and associations.

THEIR NAME AT A GLANCE

- The brain prioritizes sound into three different "listening levels." Speaking someone's name is magical because it breaks through the first level and reaches them on the second, more important level. This temporarily commandeers their attention.
- Addressing people by name is also magical because it makes them feel significant and important.
- A person's name is so important to them that the letters it contains (especially the first initial) can actually have a significant influence on many of the choices that person makes.

- A name is an essential piece of the pattern-interrupt technique that can be used to regain control when someone's emotions take over.
- Forgetting someone's name has powerfully negative effects. Use the tips in this chapter to never forget a name again.

"IF"

I was in the middle of delivering a management seminar when a man interrupted me. "I tried that," he said, "but it didn't work."

I stopped and looked his way. I actually like it when people in my seminar rooms ask tough questions, and this one was going to make a perfect segue. "What happened?"

"Well, I listened to my employee's petty complaint—politely—and when he was finished, I asked him point-blank, 'What do you suppose we should do about it?' just like you suggested."

"And . . . ?"

"And it didn't work. He stared at me blankly and said, 'I don't know. That's why I came to you.' What am I supposed to say to that?"

"Use a magic word!" To illustrate, I whisked myself over to my case, where I produced a deck of cards. I pointed at a lady toward the front and said, "One card is upside down in this deck. Do you know which one it is?"

"Me?" She laughed. "No idea."

"Well, what would you say if you did know?"

"Uh, the eight of spades?"

"Hmm, that's weird."

I opened the box, spread the cards, and sure enough, right in the middle there was a single card reversed, its blue back standing out starkly against the rest of the faceup cards. I invited her to turn it over and show everyone that it was indeed the eight of spades.

I hooked them. After the initial reaction from the group had settled down, I took advantage of the excitement and energy of the moment and delivered my main point.

"Sometimes in life people know the answer, but they just don't know that they know. Maybe they know exactly how they feel, but they're too afraid to say it out loud. You thought you had no idea what the card was until I asked you the question 'What would you say if you did know?' That question doesn't even make any sense! But it was the magic word 'if' that allowed you to think hypothetically. It took away all the pressure that was preventing you from answering me the first time. It was my magic trick that allowed you to guess the right answer, but it was the magic word 'if' that allowed you to guess at all."

I looked back at the guy with the chronic-complainer situation. "Whenever anybody says, 'I don't know,' try asking, 'What would you say if you did know?' You'd be amazed at how often it gets them to open up."

THE FOUR FACES OF PSYCHOLOGICAL RESISTANCE

Often, what we're trying to do in our communications with others can be summed up in one word: "influence." We want to influence customers to buy. We want to influence the boss to give us a raise. We want to influence our employees to be more motivated and productive.

The only problem is, no one wants to be influenced.

We all feel a compelling drive to exercise free will in our choices and our actions. So we've adopted a series of psychological resistance techniques in order to defend against the powers of persuasion. And we're *good*. More than ever, our resistance muscles are bulging and veiny because we resist thousands of advertising messages every single day. If you don't know how to say no in today's world, then you'll be broke by Wednesday.

In an amazing study done by Matthew T. Crawford, Allen R. McConnell, A. R. Lewis, and Steven J. Sherman, participants were presented with two equally matched football teams on which to gamble. When another participant (actually a plant by the researchers) said, "You definitely have to pick Team _____," the participants proceeded to choose the OPPOSITE team a whopping 76.5 percent of the time! That's the power of reverse psychology in action.

In their book *Resistance and Persuasion*, Eric Knowles and Jay Linn pose a solution to people's deep aversion of being influenced:

Resistance hounds persuasion the way friction frustrates motion. To accomplish the latter, you have to expect and, preferably, manage the former. It makes sense that those who desire to understand

persuasion should also seek to understand the nature and oper-
ation of resistance to persuasion.

They go on to identify four resistance barriers. As it turns out, the word "if" can help to magically break down each of them.

Let's say someone is trying to sell you life insurance. This life insurance policy is in your best interest, but the four faces of resistance are threatening to prevent you from making a good decision.

A great salesperson will do two things. First, they'll determine if their product is the ideal solution for you. Second, if (and *only* if) it is, then they'll help you get over the short-term resistance so you can enjoy the long-term benefits.

The salesperson already knows that this life insurance plan is a perfect fit for you. However, you're about to be a tough customer.

"Hey, have you considered buying more life insurance? I think Policy X would be a great fit for you!"

Ugh, he came at you with the hard sell. When that happens, the first face of resistance rears its ugly . . . um . . . face.

"Stop trying to *sell* me life insurance that I don't need!"

You're feeling pressured. You've recognized that you're being sold to and you're digging in your heels. This is called the "reactance" face of resistance. You feel like you're being pushed, so you're pushing back. Once you're in this mode of thinking, no matter what approach they take, you ain't budging.

If the salesperson had tried using the magic word "if" and creating a nonthreatening hypothetical situation, things may have been different. Here's what he might have said:

"If a person came to me in your exact situation, I would recommend Policy X."

Sounds harmless, doesn't it? He's not recommending any-thing to you directly. It's for some other imaginary person. "If" has just opened a door that the "reactance" face of resistance would have immediately slammed shut. Unfortunately for you, your resistance won't let you see the great deal right in front of you. Here comes the next face of resistance—"distrust."

"Well, that's just because you'd earn a fat commission! All salespeople are only out to rip people off."

This one is certainly understandable. There are some sales-people who have ulterior motives. Some would even say that the majority of salespeople are focused only on commission. I don't know the exact numbers, but I do know this—it isn't 100 percent. There's a chance that this particular salesperson is just trying to be helpful. (There is, really!)

The face of distrust tends to show up in absolutes. "All sales-people are only out to rip people off" is a perfect example of this type of blanket statement. Some more examples are: "All men are dogs," "All politicians are liars," "All lawyers are slimy."

The magic word "if" brings people away from the dangerous territory of absolutes and back into a more realistic viewpoint. Here's how the honest salesperson might use a few "ifs" to help you overcome your distrust:

"Yes, it's definitely true that some salespeople are out to rip you off. I've run across them myself. We all have. But what if there was an actual cure for cancer out there? If we wanted to tell people about it, we'd have to 'sell' the idea. Does that mean we're trying to rip people off? Of course not. Now, let's be hon-est, Policy X is no cure for cancer, but what if it is the cure for your life insurance problem?"

Nicely done, life insurance sales guy! He's gotten you past the distrust phase, but you're not done fighting yet.

"Maybe. I'm just not sure about the price." (Or any other objections you may have.)

Enter the third face of resistance. This is the time of the decision-making process when you weigh all the pros and cons a little more thoughtfully and thoroughly. As you discuss the details of Policy X with the honest salesperson, the strengths of it are appreciated, but the weaknesses are brought to light as well. It is these weaknesses that can create the face of psychological resistance known as "scrutiny." Scrutiny has a legitimate shot at ruining this for you. Fortunately, your honest salesperson is once again equipped with the magic word "if."

"If I could show you a way to get the full benefits of Policy X for an extremely affordable rate, would you do it?"

That particular line is so effective that even the dishonest salespeople have success with it. If you agree to that, then you're pretty much committed. If you say no now, you're only disagreeing with yourself. Once again, it is a sentence that is easier to say yes to because it's only hypothetical. There's no heavy weight of reality yet.

At this point, three of the faces of resistance have been overcome. It's a simple matter for your honest salesperson to lay out the facts and allow you to make the best decision. However, even though you two are now essentially in agreement about Policy X, you've still got one face of resistance to get past if you're going to enjoy the superior life insurance policy at the superior price. If your honest salesperson doesn't get you past this one, then he's failed you. You'll be forced to settle for second best.

It's the resistance face Knowles and Linn call "inertia."

The number one most difficult thing for a human being to do

is not climb Mount Everest. It's not raise a child. It's not create beautiful works of art. Psychologists tell us that the number one most difficult thing for a human being to do is to change their behavior patterns. We *hate* change.

That's why we keep our magazine subscriptions long after we've stopped reading the issues. It's why our New Year's resolutions are forgotten by January 3. It's also why we say to our life insurance salesperson, "Sounds great. I'll get back to you about this next week"—and then never do.

Inertia is the chasm between agreeing to do something and actually doing it.

Guess how your honest salesperson is going to save you from procrastination and build you a bridge across the chasm of inertia? Yup, the magic word "if." He says:

"A lot can happen in a week. What happens to your family if—God forbid—something were to happen to you between now and next week? How would you feel about your decision to put this off?"

You're now experiencing what psychologists call "anticipation of regret." In the Crawford, McConnell, Lewis, and Sherman study mentioned earlier, they added a condition of anticipated regret. Now, instead of their plant just saying, "You definitely have to pick Team _____," they also added phrases such as "because you'll kick yourself if you don't pick them and they win" or "how bad would you feel if you don't and they end up winning?"

The anticipation of regret had a dramatic effect on the decisions of participant. Before, 76.5 percent of the participants did NOT choose the recommended team. With anticipation of regret, participants completely switched their behavior and chose the recommended team more than 73 percent of the time! It seems that their resistance all but disappeared. Magic words like "if" tend to have that effect.

"IF" FOR WHEN THEY CAN'T

It was a beautiful Sunday afternoon and my family and I were driving home from church. I thought it would be a good idea to get some ice cream, so I suggested it to my wife. However, you can't just say "ice cream" when there is a two-year-old in the car and no ice cream directly within her line of sight. So, naturally I used the international parental code:

"Would you like to stop and get some I-C-E C-R-E-A-M?"

My wife immediately said yes, but Chloe asked, "Daddy, what's that spell?" Now to put this in context, "ice cream" was one of Chloe's first sight words. She could read "ice cream," spell "ice cream," and she knew everything there was to know about "ice cream."

So I dismissed her. "Come on, Chloe. You know what that means. Just sound it out."

"I can't."

This is it. This is the moment.

It happens every day, all across the world. A small child says to their parents, "I can't." An employee says to their boss, "I can't." Someone says to himself, "I can't." If there is ever a magic word that doesn't use its powers for good, it's the word "can't." Only bad things can come of this. Children miss out on life's little learning experiences, employees are less productive, and people everywhere stay neatly in their comfort zones, never stretching or growing.

So all across the world well-meaning people blurt out the retort "Yes, you CAN!" Whenever we say this, our intentions are good but our results don't always turn out so well. The problem is, we're beginning from a place of disagreement. They say "I can't," we say "Yes, you can," and they think to themselves, *No, you don't understand. I just said that I can't. Maybe you didn't hear me. Tell you what I'll do—I'll say it louder this time.* (Which they do.)

"NO, I *really* can't!"

If you push someone, their natural reaction is to push back. They'll dig in their heels and make sure that they're right and you're wrong. Try saying "Yes, you can" again and they'll really be convinced that you don't understand. They'll feel obligated to *show* you that they can't do it.

The magic word "if" is the antidote to this fruitless back-and-forth.

Instead of saying "Yes, you can" to Chloe, I tried a different approach.

"Chloe, what would you say if you did know?"

You would be amazed at how often this works—and not just for children. I once asked an employee, "What do you think about this project?" He said, "I don't really know." I used the magic word: "What would you say if you did know?" He immediately answered, "Well, if I did know, then I would probably say something about the fact that it's not really tied in to our big-picture plans. It's kind of a distraction." This is just one example of many, many "magical" turnarounds created by the word "if."

But it doesn't always work out that way. What if my daughter responded with "But, Daddy, I *don't* know"? (Which she did.)

I had to up the ante a little bit and take the hypothetical up another level. I countered with "That's not what I really meant. What I really meant was, what would I say if you asked me?"

She *immediately* responded, "Well, you'd say 'ice cream,' but *you* know."

Anytime someone comes at you with some kind of "I can't," throw the magic word "if" at them and see what happens.

Here's another great script that takes advantage of the magic word "if." I first heard this from an attorney and communication expert named Dave Frees. This one you'll want to use word for word. Pay close attention, this baby is packed with psychological encouragement.

"I know you feel like you can't, but what would happen if you did?"

Let's unpack this for a moment. This sentence begins from a place of agreement ("I know"). It makes the idea of "can't" seem far less permanent ("You *feel* like you can't"). It throws in an intentional But Eraser (refer to the chapter on "but"), which further moves them away from the idea of "can't." And finally, it closes with the magical word "if."

In the workplace, Frees goes on to say, "Because I can think of two or three ways to get this done and I'm not nearly as creative and resourceful as you are." Or "What would have to happen so that you could feel sure and confident that you could get this done by the deadline or even sooner?" Whether or not you include these depends upon your situation, of course.

Is this going to work every time? No. Clearly, nothing works 100 percent of the time. But I'll take my chances with this over a halfhearted "Yes, you can!" any day of the week.

"IF" FOR WHEN THEY COMPLAIN

You know the complaining type: nothing is good enough. Everything is miserable. And they feel it's their duty to inform you just how bad things are. All. Day. Long.

If you find yourself surrounded by workplace negativity, then it's time to put the magic word "if" to work for you.

Here are the five steps for dealing with a chronic complainer:

Step 1: Sift through all the negativity and determine what their main concerns are. I'm not ashamed to pull out a pad of paper and start making a list of their issues while they're complaining, "to make sure I get everything right." Don't allow them to repeat themselves.

Step 2: Repeat the list of grievances back, in order to confirm that you're correct.

Step 3: Quickly convert them to optimism by asking for suggested solutions instead of more problems.

Step 4: Provide a plan of action.

Step 5: Wrap it up. Complainers don't know how to end a conversation. In fact, they'll miss all the obvious social cues that you've heard enough. You must put a stop to it. Be assertive and be ultra-clear if you have to.

In theory, this all sounds lovely, but somewhere around Step 3 (when you ask for solutions) your chronic complainer says, "I don't know how to fix it. That's why I'm coming to you." That doesn't exactly sound like a quick conversion to optimism.

That's why it's time to drop an "if" bomb. Try this script:

"If I had a magic wand and could make anything in the world happen, what would you want the outcome to look like?"

The magic word "if" just solved the real problem with step three. They were unable to focus on solutions because they got hung up on the HOW. Well, you can't figure out "how" to implement a solution until you actually have a solution. You've got to focus on the "what," and that's where the "if" comes in handy.

"If I had a magic wand" sends the message: Forget about the "how" for now. Instead, let's stick with finding a "what."

Why is it so important to get them to imagine a successful outcome? Because the moment they imagine it and explain it, it becomes more likely to actually happen.

This might seem silly or overly simplistic, but don't ever underestimate the ability of the human mind to affect outcomes. The mysterious placebo effect is a prime example of the impressive power of imagination.

Research conducted by S. J. Sherman, R. B. Skov, E. F. Hervitz, and C. B. Stock at Indiana University found that when people describe a hypothetical outcome in a positive light, it will not only increase their expectations for success, it will also improve their actual performance. The hypothetical element is the key, and the word "if" brings them there.

"IF'S" DEADLY COUSIN

The flip side to the freeing motivational power of the word "if" is its deadly cousin, "then." Here are some examples of where you might find "if's" lowly relative:

- If you clean your room, then I'll give you a treat.
- If you make the sale, then I'll give you a commission.
- If you're nice to me, then I'll be nice to you.
- If you do your homework, then you'll get good grades. If you get good grades, then you'll get into college. If you get into college, then you'll get a job. If you get a job, then you'll be happy.

There are *some* instances when these "if/then" statements are perfectly appropriate. They *may* even help gain compliance and quick results. However, sometimes those quick results might end up costing you more than they're worth.

What's so deadly about "then"? Actually, lots. Here are four of the many negative effects that occur when you repeatedly combine "if" with "*then*":

T—TRANSACTIONAL

In his book *Predictably Irrational*, Dan Ariely writes brilliantly about how social norms and market norms each affect our behavior differently. Social norms are the set of beliefs and behaviors that surround our casual friendly interactions. It's how we think and feel when interacting with friends and family.

Have you ever refused payment for something because "that's just what friends do"? Does a doting grandma accept cash for babysitting her own grandchildren? Not likely. And if you offered her a fifty, she might actually get offended. In the world of social norms, $0 is greater than $50.

Market norms, on the other hand, are much more businesslike.

They usually require some kind of immediate payback. I'll give you a dollar and you'll give me that cookie. If you scratch my back, then I'll scratch yours. Think "transactional."

When our brains are engaged in market-norms thinking, we become intently focused on how and when we will be compensated for our time, treasure, and talent. Moreover, the moment market norms come into play, social norms go out the window. You can have either your heart invested in something or your wallet, but not both.

So, which one is better? Which of the two worlds do you prefer that your relationships operate in? Ultimately, that's up to you and the specific circumstance you find yourself in. Are you looking for a transaction? A quick, straightforward result with little or no creativity required? In that case, stick with market norms. Or do you want people to turn in their absolute best, creative, enthusiastic work over an extended period of time?

The evidence shows that having a market-norms mind-set will not only damage long-term relationships, it will also damage short-term results. According to Ariely: "There are many examples to show that people will work more for a cause than for cash."

All too often, we let a market-norms mentality infect the areas of our lives that should be governed by social norms. We promise our children rewards if they clean their rooms. We offer our employees incentives in exchange for good work. We pay for dinner in the hopes that we'll get a kiss at the end of a date.

Do we really want our kids to keep their rooms clean only if there's something in it for them? No! We want them to keep their rooms clean because we're a family and families help each other around the house. Do we want to have to reward our employees every time they show up to work on time? Of course not; that should be a given. Do we want our romantic interactions to feel like prostitution? How unromantic is that?

Market norms may foster compliance, but social norms foster engagement. Compliance is a short-term result, and engagement is for the long haul. Look at your current situation. Would you prefer compliance or engagement? Unfortunately, most if/then statements are transactional and not relational. They drag the mind-set back to the world of market norms, block out social norms, and therefore snuff out the engagement, creativity, and motivation of the people who you interact with.

This is especially important for anyone in a leadership position. Mark Sanborn, author of *You Don't Need a Title to Be a Leader*, offers this leadership test: "If you had no title or ability to reward or penalize others, could you still get them to follow you?"

"If/then" statements are transactional. In most cases, we need to be more relational in our dealings with others.

H—HEROIN-LIKE

"If's" deadly cousin, "then," is a bit like heroin. Hear me out on this one. It'll make sense, I promise.

"If/Then" High

When someone is rewarded for a job well done, it's a pretty exciting moment. In fact, their brain literally experiences a bit of a "high." When a dangling carrot has finally been snagged, the nucleus accumbens—the brain's "reward center"—fires away. This, incidentally, is the same part of the brain that would light up if you were to shoot heroin.

"If/Then" Tolerance

The problem with "if/then" rewards like this is that they aren't good enough next time. Next time, you need a little bit more of a reward if you're going to reach the same level of motivational high. Think about this: if you got a "Caught Doing Good Certificate" at work, that might make you feel pretty good, right? However, what if you already had two hundred of them sitting on your desk? Not so inspiring anymore, is it? People will build up a tolerance to "if/then" rewards in the same way they build up a tolerance to heroin.

"If/Then" Overdose

We know it's possible to overdose on heroin, but is it possible to overdose on "if/then" rewards? Just ask those members of Generation Y who have experienced this firsthand. The self-esteem movement created a situation where an entire generation has been over-rewarded. They've been given trophies for fifth place. The F's have been taken off their papers because they made kids feel bad. In trying to make every kid feel special, the very essence of special has been destroyed. I've consulted with several companies that simply will not hire recent college graduates who are members of Generation Y. They claim that these individuals feel overly entitled and lack any sense of company loyalty. They've OD'd.

I've found that Gen Yers aren't as "unhire-able" as some might suggest. I think they simply are forcing us to update and improve our style of leadership. We must learn to lead through relationships and collaboration rather than control. We must learn to build trust and respect instead of trying to instill fear. Market norms are failing us. Our only hope is to go to Reward

Rehab, reestablish social norms in the workplace, and inject more human connection into a generation that is starved for it.

"If/Then" Junkies

Like heroin, rewards are addictive. "If/then" statements can create "if/then" junkies. These people will sabotage others or cut corners in order to receive their "reward fix" faster.

We're using market norms to motivate people, and then getting upset when they don't follow social norms! Respecting others? Doing a job well just for the sake of doing a job well? Showing up early and staying late? Loyalty? Integrity? These virtues have no place in the world of market norms.

E—EXTRINSIC

In the "because" chapter, we learned about the power of intrinsic motivation—the kind of motivation that comes from within. The people who are motivated in this way do what they do because they "love to," or maybe even because they feel "called to."

The problem is, "if's" deadly cousin, "then," forces people down into the depths of extrinsic motivation. Not good. Here's what Edward Deci, professor of psychology at the University of Rochester, cofounder of Self-Determination Theory, and all-around human-motivation expert, wrote in a lengthy-titled paper in 1999:

> When organizations opt for the use of rewards to control behavior, the rewards are likely to be accompanied by greater surveillance, evaluation, and competition, all of which have also been found to undermine intrinsic motivation. (Deci & Ryan, 1985)

It's important to take a moment to note that the rewards themselves are not what are doing the damage. It's the person's expectation of the reward. It's "if's" deadly cousin, "then," that is causing all the trouble.

Want your employees, students, and children to be intrinsically motivated? My advice would be to lay off the "if/then" rewards.

N—NEARSIGHTED

In *Drive: The Surprising Truth about What Motivates Us*, Daniel H. Pink discusses this negative aspect of "if/then" reward statements:

> *Rewards can limit the breadth of our thinking. But extrinsic motivators—especially tangible, "if-then" ones—can also reduce the depth of our thinking. They can focus our sights on only what's immediately before us rather than what's off in the distance. . . . Greatness and nearsightedness are incompatible. Meaningful achievement depends on lifting one's sights and pushing toward the horizon.*

As we have seen, "if" has incredible motivating potential when deftly used. Don't mess up the party by inviting "then."

IT'S NOT ALL BAD

Monica Cornetti, a speaker and author on the topic of "gamification," is not yet ready to count out extrinsic motivation. "Most people would agree that intrinsic motivation is the motivator that you're looking for more so than extrinsic motivation, however . . ." She goes on to contend that sometimes, in some situations, if/then rewards may still have a place.

Her work in gamification gives her a glimpse into what drives people. "Gamification is the process of applying game psychology to non-game settings in an effort to motivate people to do the things that we want or need them to do," she says.

Games certainly can be motivating. Some can be downright addictive. Many of us have had the experience of being "hooked" on a computer game, a puzzle, or some other form of play.

Before millions of zombie-faced gamers were staring at their softly glowing devices playing Angry Birds or Candy Crush; before Mr. Rubik's colored cubes sent the multitudes into mad fits of "JUST ONE MORE TWIST!"; and even before the ancients faced off across the first checkerboards, the brain was wired to love games. The "work" of solving a problem or the reward of winning is like candy to the brain. But can the addictive nature of games be applied to motivating human beings in more productive areas of life? And if so, should it?

"What are our objectives? What are we trying to achieve? What behaviors will we need from individuals so that we know we will be able to achieve those objectives? And how do we get people to do those behaviors?" Cornetti asks.

For example, is it possible to use game elements like "if/then" rewards to get kids to become obsessed with algebra? Or to solve a medical problem that has plagued the world's top PhDs for fifteen years? Or to completely wipe the idea of "work" off the face of the planet?

Gamification pioneer Yu-kai Chou says absolutely yes. However, the "if/then" extrinsic rewards aren't doing all the heavy lifting. In his "Octalysis" model, he outlines eight different elements that make games addictive and how each of the elements can be applied to non-gaming scenarios. The "if/then" rewards are only one of the eight core motivators—and one of the weaker ones at that.

The point is, "if/then" motivators can be effective in the right situation with the right person for the right reasons. However, the problems come when we focus exclusively on extrinsic motivators. Why do we tend to spend 90 percent of our time using a technique that is only 10 percent effective?

Spend the majority of your time cultivating long-term intrinsic motivation in yourself and in others and use "if/then" motivators sparingly—like a spice.

For the complete interview with Monica Cornetti and a video of Yu-kai Chou explaining his complete Octalysis model, visit MagicWordsBook.com/games.

"IF" AT A GLANCE

- The magic behind "if" lies in its ability to engage the imagination.
- "If" can help to remove barriers to creativity, overcome the four faces of psychological resistance, and increase the likelihood of a positive outcome.
- "If/then" statements must be used with extreme caution.

"HELP"

Early in my magic career, my focus was on what I could do that my audience could not. My patter consisted of such gems as, "Here's what I'm going to do . . ." and "Watch as I turn these metal discs into quarters." Every single magic book I read taught me to call my audiences "spectators." Dictionary.com says a spectator is "a person who is present at and views a spectacle. A person who looks on or watches; onlooker; observer." In other words, there, but detached from the action. Totally uninvolved.

My first "shows" consisted of sitting on the stairs in my parents' house waiting for just the right moment to interrupt their dinner guests with my latest magic trick. My approach was very much "Hurry up and pick a card so you can get back to focusing on me," while they were probably thinking, *Hurry up and find it so we can get back to our conversation.*

Both of us started to change our minds after I discovered what is undoubtedly the greatest card trick of all time.

When I first came across it, the text said that it was the card trick to end all card tricks. Sounded pretty good to me. The only problem was that there was no spectator in this trick—only a participant. Reluctantly, I gave it a try.

"I need your help," I said to one of my mother's friends. I instructed her to randomly deal cards one at a time into two facedown piles. "However you want to do this is fine. Just feel the vibes of the cards and use the Force."

When she finished the entire deck, the cards were turned over, and to everyone's amazement (especially the participant's), she had dealt all the red cards into one pile and all the black cards into the other. Everyone was stunned.

It took a few years, but slowly it dawned on me why people enjoyed this trick so much. It wasn't the elegant secret behind the trick. It wasn't the powerful effect. It was something that would change the course of my entire career forever: "audience participation."

A seismic shift had occurred. Suddenly, I went from being the "mage from the stage" to being a "guide from the side." It was no longer about showing people tricks. Instead, it was about leading them through an experience. The results were immediate and obvious, and the word "help" was the cornerstone.

True positive influence is not about being a "mage from the stage." You don't want to be the guru at the top of the mountain with all the answers. If you did have all the answers, then people would be coming to you for all the answers. *Constantly.* When you solve problems and provide answers for people, they don't need to learn how to do it for themselves. They need you.

THE PROBLEM WITH BEING NEEDED

Dale Carnegie says that we all have a deep need for significance. We all want to feel needed—for a little while. The problems come when otherwise healthy and talented people become totally dependent on us.

Ultimately, your job as a parent is to make sure your children grow up, mature, and stop needing you, isn't it? Your job as a manager is to empower your employees so you don't have to do their jobs for them. As a leader, you want your organization to survive long after you've gone. Being needed is a temporary thing.

Maybe we don't even want our bosses to need us! I know it sounds like backward thinking, but if you're not replaceable, then you're not promotable. Very often I'll hear my consulting clients say something like "She's so good that I can't promote her. I *need her* right where she is."

The biggest problem with being needed is that it requires someone else to be needy. Instead of a dependent or even independent mind-set, Stephen Covey espouses the concept of interdependence in his book *The 7 Habits of Highly Effective People*:

Life is, by nature, highly interdependent. . . . If I am physically interdependent, I am self-reliant and capable, but I also realize that you and I working together can accomplish far more than, even at my best, I could accomplish alone. If I am emotionally interdependent, I derive a great sense of worth within myself, but I also recognize the need for love, for giving, and for receiving love from others. If I am intellectually interdependent, I realize that I need the best thinking of other people to join with my own.

Interdependence is great for our personal relationships, but business is different, right? Surely we want our customers to need us, don't we? Amanda Palmer doesn't think so. In her widely viewed TED talk, she paints her vision for the future of the music industry. While the major record labels are trying to squash online piracy and ultimately force customers to *need* them, Palmer is giving her music away for free on the Internet as often as she can in an effort to build connection.

How can free possibly be a good idea? You can't live on free. Can you?

The way Palmer describes it, she doesn't survive on her album sales. (Obviously.) Instead, she survives by not being afraid or ashamed of asking her connections for help when help is needed.

Case in point: when her record label was only able to sell twenty-five thousand units of her album, their transactional mind-set considered it a bust and they moved on. As it turns out, twenty-five thousand units isn't a whole lot to a record company. But Amanda Palmer saw those twenty-five thousand units as a whole bunch of new connections. They aren't transactions. They're relationships.

Sometime later, when she needed $100,000 to release an album on her own, she asked her twenty-five thousand connections for help. Her relational approach ended up garnering almost $1.2 million in support—the single most successful music crowdfunding campaign to date.

The media was dumbfounded. They saw a music industry that was in a tailspin because of online piracy, yet here was a woman who encouraged free music and somehow she found a way to make people pay for her music.

She responded to the criticism, "I didn't make them. I asked them. And through the very act of asking people, I connected with them. And when you connect with them, people want to help you."

Is that true? Do people really want to help?

I can see why a telemarketer would vehemently disagree. It can be exhausting to the human spirit to be rejected fifty times per day. I know because when I first started booking myself as a magician, I didn't have any other ideas as to how to get gigs. I picked up the phone and dialed like I was getting paid by the number. People seem to have no problem hanging up on telemarketers. The moment I was identified as someone who was selling something, I would hear the dial tone.

Through trial and error, I eventually and organically changed my conversation style from something like "Can I please speak to the person in charge of hiring entertainment?" to something like "Hi, [so and so], my name is Tim. I have kind of a weird question. I was wondering if you could help me out?"

No one ever said no to my request for help. Sure, they sometimes asked qualifying questions like "What kind of help?" before they made any commitments. But on the chart of who said what, the biggest piece of the pie was taken by the folks who appeared willing and even eager to help.

Perhaps it's because I used their name (when possible). Maybe it was because of the curiosity I built with the phrase "kind of a weird question." Or maybe it was the magic word "help." Suddenly, I was not someone who was robotically farming for transactions. I was someone who allowed himself to become vulnerable. I trusted them with my ego, and they didn't let me down. A connection—however small—was made.

Think about how you feel when someone asks you for help.

"You are motivated because you feel like you are part of something bigger than yourself," says Yu-kai Chou, the gamification and human-motivation expert we met in the chapter on "If." "It makes you feel important, like people are depending on you."

Of course, there are also times when you don't feel that sense of togetherness when others come to you for help. Instead, you feel put out. You feel taken advantage of. You feel used. What went wrong?

The times you don't respond with an eager desire to help are the times when human connection has either broken down or never been established in the first place. That's why when asking others for help, it must be an authentic and vulnerable plea and not just a tool to get what you want.

PLURAL PRONOUNS

Good call-center employees are experts at taking an irate, complaining customer and turning them into a problem-solving ally in a very short amount of time. (Bad call-center employees end up quitting their jobs after a very short amount of time.) One of their most successful strategies is to sprinkle plural pronouns throughout the conversation.

"I completely understand how you feel, sir, and we can absolutely help you with that. Let's take a look at your account and see what we can do for you."

Words like "let's" and "we" are like mini magic words that help build connection. It's subtle, but it's strong. What you're saying is, "I'm on your side. It's not you versus me. We're in this together."

One of the strongest connections two human beings can have is being aligned against a common enemy. This is why the "good cop/bad cop" strategy works so well. The target of the strategy and the good cop are a team working toward the same mission of saving the target from the bad cop.

When asking for help, you must be perceived as the ally and not the enemy. Using plural pronouns will do that for you.

WHY MANAGERS DON'T ASK FOR HELP AS OFTEN AS THEY SHOULD

In the world of management, they don't call it "asking for help." They call it "delegating."

When I do trainings for people in management and leadership positions, I'm fond of asking them two simple questions. I start with the easy one.

"Should we delegate?"

Absolutely. They all nod their heads in agreement, as though the question were the biggest no-brainer in America. Then I pose the follow-up.

"Do we delegate like we should?"

Silence.

They shake their heads while looking around the room to make sure they're not the only ones. The answer is clear: we don't.

"Why not?"

If "help" is such a magical word, and if the connection it creates is such a beautiful thing, then why don't we say it more?

The first reason is that it makes us vulnerable! We live in a culture that values independence and being able to "look out for #1." If we ask for help, then somehow we feel like we've failed.

Managers don't say that, though. Instead, some will say that they're afraid of appearing bossy or confrontational. Others will say that they don't want other people doing their tasks and potentially stealing their jobs. The most common response, though?

"Because I can do it better and faster myself!"

They don't want to give up control. They don't want to sit around and train somebody to do a task and just end up correcting their work five times anyway. It's just easier, faster, and more efficient for the managers to forget about delegating and simply do everything themselves.

In the short term, they're absolutely right. Life goes on and tasks get completed. However, in the long term, connection and empowerment get lost, and employee engagement disappears without a trace.

CHLOE'S THREE LAWS OF DELEGATION

My daughter Chloe taught me a lot about how to delegate a task in such a way that it fosters engagement instead of embitterment and results in action instead of aggression.

It started when she wouldn't finish all her Cheerios. Day after day there was a soggy mess at the bottom of the bowl.

So every day, I gave her fewer and fewer Cheerios.

Finally, she noticed. "Daddy, I want *more* Cheerios!" At this point, it almost didn't matter how much I gave her. A familiar pattern quickly developed where she would never finish her Cheerios, yet every day she'd whine for more.

I tried using some logic. "Honey, eat what I gave you, and I'll be happy to give you more. It's not like there's a Cheerio famine going on, I just don't want any to go to waste."

She knew exactly what to say next. Kids always do. "Daddy, let me pour my *own* bowl."

My knee-jerk reaction was to say no. It would make a mess. It would take too long. I can do it faster and better myself. Sound familiar, managers?

Fortunately, a phrase ran through my mind at that moment—a phrase that I've since dubbed "Chloe's 1st Law of Delegation."

Law #1: If They Ask for the Task, Then Give It to Them

We all need a little bit of challenge in our lives. Famed Hungarian psychology professor Mihaly Csikszentmihalyi famously named the sweet spot between being bored and being overwhelmed. He called it "flow." Flow is where you are the most engaged, motivated, and happiest. You might call it "being in the zone." The best leaders recognize the importance of pushing others toward flow. They delegate enough to challenge, but not so much that people become resentful or overworked.

If someone is asking you for a task, then guess what? They're BORED! Absolutely give them the task (if it is possible to do so) and make a mental note that you're not challenging that person enough. You probably should have given them this task a long time ago.

We all have doubts and fears that stifle our capabilities. A good amount of time passes between the moment we become ready for a task and the moment we *realize* that we're ready for that task. Isn't it also true that even when we do recognize our own capabilities, sometimes it takes us a while to build up the courage to ask for a task? A great leader can see things in us that we can't even see in ourselves.

So know that when someone volunteers for a task, under the surface is a lot of time that has already passed leading up to this moment. Opportunities to effectively challenge this person have already been missed. Don't worry, though—you're onto them now, just like I was onto Chloe. I reached into the cabinet for the Cheerios box and a bowl. I also got her a spoon and the jug of milk from the fridge. Then I put it all on the floor—which brings me to Chloe's 2nd Law of Delegation.

Law #2: Allow People to Fail SAFELY

I didn't get her set up on the table because that's where the laptop was. If I put her up there, then I might be the one crying over spilled milk!

Of course, you want to stretch people's perceived limits (1st Law), but you don't want to break them! Don't give a new employee the company's largest client account to practice on, and don't let a med student perform life-or-death surgery if they have no experience with such tasks. They'll be stretched, all right, but if and when they fail, it could absolutely destroy their motivation to ever try again.

The scene was set for Chloe to fail safely, and she did not disappoint. Now, she'd seen me pour Cheerios dozens if not hundreds of times. I'm not sure where she picked up her rather unorthodox technique. She started by opening the box of Cheerios (which was chest height for her). Then she stood behind it and sank both arms into the Cheerios up to her shoulders. She scooped out two armfuls of Cheerios like an excavator, waddled over to the bowl, and . . . bombs away.

Here's a piece of advice I'm sure you'll need when following Chloe's 2nd Law of Delegation:

Resist the urge to jump in and correct

For some, it's a powerful urge. For others, it's a habit or even a compulsion. I had a frustrated woman confront me once: "I can't get my teenage boys to clean their rooms! Do you have any magic words for that, Magic Boy? It's driving me crazy. I'm constantly cleaning up after their mess!"

Maybe it's hard for them to grab hold of the task because you're still clutching onto it for dear life. A task can have only one owner. When you jump in and correct, or when you take over a job outright, you are taking back ownership. In this mom's case, because she took over, the consequences for not cleaning their rooms were: CLEAN ROOMS!

The compulsion to correct mistakes is understandable, and yet it is also manageable. The reason Chloe's 2nd Law exists is that failure is a great teacher. When you jump in and correct, you rob them of the opportunity to fail. We saw what happens when failure is removed during the self-esteem movement. Since the eighties and nineties, every child has been given trophies just for "participating." Every child is celebrated because of their "potential." Failure is systematically removed and replaced with a mantra of "everyone is special."

You should allow people to fail, but only if they are likely to fail forward. Failure can be a teacher, but it can also be a tragedy. If a teenager experiments with heavy drugs and is killed, then that's not a lesson. That's a tragedy. It's your responsibility to know the difference.

Before you delegate any task, you must answer the following question:

Which is more important, the task or the relationship?

All tasks seem important at the time. Sure, I wanted Chloe to eat her Cheerios so we could get her to school on time. However, my relationship with her was even more important.

This isn't always the case. For example, a gentleman in one

of my seminars said, "I work in high-pressure pipe fittings. If one of my guys is off by one half of 1 percent, then people die." A nurse said, "If we make one mistake with someone's prescription, then that person's life may be in danger." Here, the task is more important than the relationship. If failure will result in tragedy instead of a teachable moment, then you have an obligation to jump in and make any corrections you see fit.

Spilling Cheerios and being ten minutes late to school? That's not exactly a tragedy. So I let Chloe fill her bowl until she had the largest mound of Cheerios I had ever seen. Next came the milk. Chloe instantly flipped the jug 180 degrees. Milk shot out, hit the side of the bowl, and another mess was made.

Finally, after cleaning up the spilled milk and Cheerios and trying again, she sat at the table with *her* breakfast in front of her. Over and over she squealed, "I did it! I did it!"

Wouldn't you know it? That kid ate every single bite of Mount Cheerios.

Not only that, but for months afterward the same scene would play out every morning. She would set the table and pour everyone's favorite cereal. She knew the bowls and spoons to set out for her sister and her parents. She knew just the right amount of milk that everyone preferred. She took pride in her work, and she did an amazing job. She had become empowered and the task had become hers. Best of all, it was one less part of our morning routine that Daddy had to worry about.

Law #3: Bring People Problems, Not Solutions

The brain is wired to solve problems. Give it the solution and it's instantly bored. Give it a question or a problem and it does the neurological equivalent of a happy dance.

I've seen this happen literally thousands of times. If I showed you a really good magic trick, at first you'd find it wonderful, delightful, and magical. It would intrigue your mind. Maybe it would even keep you up at night. Then you'd beg me for the secret.

But I'll never tell, because nothing is worse than the expression of someone who finally gets to pull back the curtain and peer inside the secret of a magic trick that had previously bamboozled them. Their faces fall and their hearts sink. They feel disappointed and let down. They hate me for allowing them to recklessly throw away their own brain candy.

Had I told Chloe exactly how to pour Cheerios, she would not have ended up with the same level of engagement in the task. She may have been compliant (after a sure power struggle), but never engaged. She was proud of herself for conquering the task. She owned it.

The next time you've got a task you need someone to do, any task, don't say the usual "Here's what needs to be done and here are the instructions for how you're going to do it." Instead, bring your people together and say, "We have a problem and I need your help to solve it." Then present the problem that your task solves and brainstorm with them.

One of three things is going to happen. The first is that they'll all decide on the same exact task that you wanted them to do in the first place! However, that's not a waste of time because their brain was engaged and challenged. A possible solution was found, and they can't wait to see if "their idea" is going to work! Discipline becomes very different and much easier in these situations, too. If they slack off, you don't have to lay down the law and say, "Hey! Didn't I tell you to do this?" Instead, you can say, "Hey, didn't YOU say you were going to do this?" You're not angry, you're disappointed. And as any kid will tell you, a parent's disappointment is a much more powerful motivating force than a parent's anger.

However, they may not come up with the solution you had in mind, which may require some coaching on your part. Simply bring up the problems that you see and let the discussion right itself and get back on course. Here's a hint: if you can't poke any holes in their plan, then guess what? Their idea is just as good as yours, only different! Let them try their idea and see what happens. They will reward you with a level of motivation that you haven't seen from them before.

The third alternative is that they come with a solution that is not only different from yours, but better! Your staff sees things differently than you do as their manager. They're on the front lines engaging in their work every day. They have valuable perspective and insight that you should be tapping into. Don't ever make the mistake of believing that you know best before even giving the other person a chance to open up their mouth. You never know, they just might surprise you. This is the beauty of communication. This is the reward of becoming vulnerable. This is the reason we ask for help.

"HELP" AT A GLANCE

- The magic word "help" fosters engagement and interdependence in those who hear it.

- A proper request for help moves people to behave according to social norms and makes them feel important—like they are part of something larger than themselves.
- Make use of plural pronouns while asking for help.
- Delegate tasks with Chloe's "Three Laws of Delegation" in mind.
- Asking for help requires vulnerability, which is a powerful force in creating connection and rapport between individuals.

"THANKS"

Howard Thurston, one of the most famous magicians in the history of magic, began every show by standing behind the curtain waiting for it to be raised. Although the audience couldn't see him yet, he still considered this moment to be the most important of his entire show. This was the moment he recited his mantra of thanks:

I'm grateful because these people come to see me. They make it possible for me to make my living. I love my audience. I love my audience. I love my audience.

Even though his audience never heard him utter these words, the effect of his gratitude was still profound. In fact, Mr. Thurston credits the success of his forty-year, multimillion-dollar, globetrotting career to this one core practice.

Steffanie Fox's hair salon, however, is a more typical example. I met the owner of Stylz by Steffanie after a speaking engagement just south of Boston. She and her team of hairdressers make it a habit to send handwritten thank-you cards to each and every new client who comes through the salon's doors. Steffanie is clearly passionate about her work and grateful for her clients and customers.

"I certainly believe anything you do to recognize people will make you stand out from the rest."

She's right, but why? Isn't saying thanks just common courtesy? Doesn't everyone do it?

Apparently not. What surprises me is that most businesses don't bother to say thanks to their customers. And most bosses don't say thanks to their employees. In fact, most people anywhere don't say thanks often enough.

I asked hundreds of people via email a single question: "Does your boss say thanks?" Most did not respond (perhaps an implied no?). Of those who did, instead of sending the positive anecdotes I was expecting, many reported horror stories of ungrateful bosses.

For example, I heard from Dave, a video producer in Detroit, who said his TV station's management had said thanks to him only once in over thirty years—and he had to achieve something rather extraordinary to "earn" it.

That kind of ingratitude is hard to overcome. It damages relationships and crushes morale. Philosopher David Hume once wrote: "Of all the crimes that human creatures are capable of committing, the most horrid and unnatural is ingratitude."

He's right. Survey after survey shows that one of the top reasons people quit their jobs is because of a poor relationship with their boss or because their boss doesn't show enough appreciation. Ingratitude is such a repulsive and unlikable trait that no one wants to be around an ungrateful person, let alone work for one.

The good news is, the bosses who do say thanks not only keep their employees around longer, but they also enjoy increased productivity. Shawn Achor, author of *The Happiness Advantage*, cites, "Coal miners who feel appreciated by their bosses increase their productivity by 30 percent and happy employees show three times greater levels of creativity."

Here are some ways I've seen bosses say thanks creatively:

Heather Taylor of MyCorporation.com says about her boss, Deborah Sweeney, "Every month in celebration of a job well done, we'll receive emails calling out each member of the team for their helpful contributions as well as treats, bagels on Fridays, catered lunches, and extra coffee incentives for everyone!"

One of Weaving Influence's contractors enthusiastically shared how founder Becky Robinson is constantly showing appreciation. "She will Tweet of her appreciation, text, share on Facebook, and write blog posts about her team."

I read one of her blog posts. Robinson took the time to mention each contractor by name and list some of their positive attributes. Whenever anyone commented on the post, Robinson quickly offered even more words of thanks and appreciation.

Public displays of thanks like this seem to go over well.

Leslie Friedman, employee at the Houstonian Hotel, Club & Spa in Houston, Texas, told me about her boss, Jim Mills. "[He] expresses his thanks to me in a very open way. Each month all employees are recognized with a 'Hooray for You!' celebration for those whose work anniversaries fall in that month. Everyone is encouraged to recognize their peers, bosses, and friends, but it is most rewarding when a boss publicly recognizes (thanks) those that work for him/her, in front of everyone.

"Jim has thanked me for my efforts, saying I've achieved more publicity for the campus than we've ever had, and for my being creative and persistent. In doing so in front of my peers and other managers, it speaks 'thank you' quite loudly."

However, retired university administrator Carol Gee's ex-boss wins the ultimate "thankful prize." "She showed she appreciated me with unexpected gifts . . . like a vacation to Aruba." Not too shabby.

Of course, your "thank-yous" don't have to be creative (or expensive!) in order for them to be effective. Most of the comments I received were from people like Mike Kennedy from Talent Analytics Corp.: "My boss, Greta Roberts, has frequently thanked me for my contributions, as she is the most gracious boss I'll ever have. A thank-you goes a long way in terms of productivity and job satisfaction. I'm a very loyal employee."

Mike believes that Greta "stands out" because of her thankfulness. "I've worked for bosses who rarely, if ever, thanked their employees. I have a greater appreciation for the effective management Greta displays."

Over and over I noticed employees commenting that hearing a simple "thanks" makes them feel respected, loyal, happier, more purposeful, more productive, and more engaged in their work. And it seemed that the more often they heard this particular magic word, the better.

BETTER THAN MONEY?

Gail Elmore has been a volunteer for the Massachusetts Hugh O'Brian Youth Leadership organization for twelve years. She helps young people build the skills and confidence necessary to become leaders in the community. "I have been fortunate to be able to devote most of my adult life to volunteering. The many 'thank-yous' I have gotten through the years is what continually motivates me to do service."

What motivates someone to devote their time and talent to an organization for more than a decade without expectation of monetary reward? I think maybe it has something to do with the meaning of life. Viktor Frankl, the famous psychologist, Holocaust survivor, and author of *Man's Search for Meaning*, penned: "Man's main concern is not to gain pleasure or to avoid pain but rather to see a meaning in his life."

How often you hear the word "thanks" is a measuring stick for the amount of meaning in your life. A "thanks" lets you know that you're contributing to the life of another person in a meaningful way. Why is contribution so important to our sense of purpose?

According to author Brendon Burchard in his book *The Charge: Activating the 10 Human Drives That Make You Feel Alive*:

At the end of our lives, when we're looking back and wondering about the meaning of it all, we'll wonder if we mattered. To discover the answer, we'll look uniquely to our connections (our loved ones and those we influenced) and to our contributions. But even as we evaluate and reflect on our connections, we're really thinking about what we contributed to those connections. We're wondering whether we gave of ourselves to our relationships, whether we loved fully and openly and honestly. We're wondering whether we gave others the time, attention, acceptance, and affection they deserved from us. We're wondering, essentially, what we contributed to the world and to those around us. In the end, that's how we gauge the meaning of our lives.

You can get paid to do just about anything. Just go to fiverr.com and see all the crazy things people will do for a little bit of money. But there are fewer tasks in this world that will result in you receiving a heartfelt thanks. When it comes to determining the value you're contributing and therefore the meaning in your life, a "thanks" is a far better measuring stick than money.

Maybe this is why we crave it so much. Or maybe it's because of the positivity ratio.

THE POSITIVITY RATIO

The research of Dr. Barbara Fredrickson points to a pretty clear conclusion. We all need to hear "thank you" . . . a lot. For all the reasons listed above, plus one more:

According to her findings, human beings need to experience three positive emotions for every one negative emotion in order to flourish. John Gottman, the famed marriage expert, suggests that the ratio is closer to five to one, and other psychologists have placed that ratio as high as seven to one. Tim Grahl, an author and blogger, writes: "And while there's no scientific study that's been done on this, I think we can all agree that most writers need to receive about 50 good reviews to recover from a single bad one."

So despite all the magical power of a "thank you," perhaps its best use is to fill the deep void of any thankless interpersonal relationship. In fact, gratitude is critical to healthy relationships.

Gottman says, "Commitment implies . . . nurturing gratitude." Jeffrey Froh, professor of psychology at Hofstra University and coauthor of *Making Grateful Kids*, called gratitude the "social glue [that] strengthens relationships." The magic word "thanks" brings us together, and a lack of the word "thanks" drives us apart.

HOW CAN PEOPLE BE SO UNGRATEFUL?

If I asked you to think of a stereotypically ungrateful person, you might conjure an image of a sullen teenager from a wealthy family. Someone who has everything he or she could ever need, someone with no responsibilities, and yet someone who has an enormous sense of entitlement and a complete lack of gratitude. You might picture them rolling their eyes when asked to take out the trash and responding with a bored "Whatevs, Dad. Just gimme the keys to the Porsche."

How can this happen? How can someone who lives a life of unmatched abundance (like most Americans, as compared with the rest of the world) not express heartfelt gratitude toward every blessing that comes their way? In short, how can we be so ungrateful?

We're actually not as ungrateful as it may seem. People are

thankful every day, but we tend to remember the ingratitude. Froh says that while it's true that some people are born with naturally ungrateful personalities, the more likely cause for the strains of ingratitude that lie in all of us is our brain's phenomenal ability to adapt. We get used to things, and suddenly we don't feel thankful for them anymore. We begin to take them for granted. A grateful person, however, will slow down the process of adaptation and actually take the time to smell the roses, or notice the beautiful sunset, or express appreciation to an employee.

And for those who do, recent research has revealed some incredible surprise benefits. For example, according to Dr. Robert Emmons, grateful people:

- live longer (about seven years longer than ungrateful people—on average)
- feel less physical pain
- exercise more
- sleep better
- are healthier
- are happier (a full 25 percent happier, according to one study)
- are less stressed
- are more generous
- are less depressed
- make better doctors and nurses
- have more energy
- are more social
- are more optimistic
- experience more overall life satisfaction

- experience less anxiety and fear
- have more ability to experience pleasure
- tend to show a positive recall bias (they remember more pleasant memories than unpleasant ones)

With incredible benefits to both the giver and the receiver, the word "thanks" appears to be just as magical as Thurston himself.

SAYING "THANKS" MORE

It's true that a grateful personality can be cultivated—even if you're a Scrooge-like ingrate. You can start by saying "thanks" more and meaning it.

Or maybe you don't even have to mean it. The concept of embodied cognition suggests that our physical bodies affect our thoughts. Just like smiling enough will make you start to feel happier, and clenching your fists will create stress and tension, by physically speaking words like "thank you," "blessed," and "abundant" aloud, and by making gestures associated with thanksgiving—such as "prayer hands," bowing, or placing your hand over your heart—your body sends signals to your brain encouraging it to produce more of the grateful feeling.

Be careful with this "fake it till you make it" strategy, though. I'd only recommend it for expressing your thanks to things such as a beautiful sunrise, the universe, or God—not to other people. A cardinal rule of communicating with other human beings is *Authenticity trumps everything.* If you try to "fake it till you make it" with another human being, they will spot you as a phony and you'll end up doing more harm than good.

Instead, challenge yourself to keep a daily handwritten gratitude journal for thirty days. Write down at least one thing you
are grateful for every day, and never repeat an item. If that's too
much for you, try naming things aloud as you commute to and
from work. Meditate. Pray. Do whatever it takes to start feeling
more thankfulness.

When you notice it beginning to work, you can graduate to
expressing thankfulness outwardly toward others. Activities
like regularly writing thank-you cards or conducting a "gratitude
visit" to someone for whom a sincere thank-you is long overdue
can also help you to cultivate more gratitude within yourself.
(Make sure you bring a box or two of tissues along on your gratitude visit.)

THE FIVE COMPONENTS OF AN
EFFECTIVE "THANKS"

Well-known gratitude researcher Jeffrey Froh was kind enough
to share these five key elements of an effective thank-you during
my interview with him:

1. **Be timely.**

It's never too late to express thanks to someone. That said,
the sooner the better—especially if you're hoping to reinforce
the behavior that you're thanking the person for.

2. **Compliment the attributes of the benefactor.**

"Thank you for listening to me the other night. You are such
a good listener, and I really appreciate that about you." Or
"Thank you for the card and gift. You are such a thoughtful

person." Allow the thank-you to extend past the deed, and let it also be about the person behind the deed.

3. Recognize the intent of the benefactor.

This is the heart of an authentic thank-you. Recognizing intent acknowledges that they did something nice for you, and it acknowledges that their good deed was premeditated. "Thanks. I know you didn't have to help me move my furniture to my new place. It's good to know people still offer to help just out of the goodness of their heart."

4. Recognize the costs to the benefactor.

Whenever people do something nice for us, they give up time, money, or energy that could have been spent doing something for themselves. Tell them that you appreciate that. "Listen, I know you left your meeting early just to come down here. It means a lot that you're putting aside your priorities for mine. Thank you."

5. Articulate the benefits.

Finally, share with them the result of their kind act. "Because of the generous support from you and others, we were able to raise four thousand dollars for needy families in our community. This money will make a big difference in their lives this holiday season. Thank you!"

CREATING A "THANKS" CULTURE

Whether you are a member of an organization or a family, if you've read this far then you probably want to create more of a "thanks" culture within that group. Here's how you can do it.

It Begins with You

It's always best to lead by example. Follow the suggestions above in order to feel more gratitude and say "thanks" more often. There's an old Turkish saying: "The fish starts stinking at the head." Don't allow ingratitude to creep into your group through you.

Get Them Involved

One November, I gave myself a thankful challenge. My daughter Chloe helped me decorate a fall scene, including a Thanksgiving turkey (made from the outline of her tiny hand). We put it into a picture frame, and every day I wrote on the glass with a dry-erase marker something that I was thankful for. And every day she would ask me what I wrote on the turkey. Not only did this keep me accountable to my challenge, but it also allowed for some amazingly touching and teachable moments.

BPOD

This stands for "best part of the day." The idea is simple. During a meeting or an evening meal, allow each person to share their BPOD. This encourages people to focus on the good things that we're thankful for instead of the not-so-good things that we'd rather complain about.

There is a great website called 100happydays.com that encourages a similar practice.

The "Thank-You System"

Here's an idea submitted by Laney Lyons that any school, company, or family can immediately use to create a more thankful culture.

Everyone gets three laminated "thank you" cards at the beginning of the week with the understanding that they must give them to anyone who does something worthy of a little extra appreciation. The person with the most thank-you cards at next week's meeting wins a small prize. If a person doesn't give away all three of their thank-you cards, then they are disqualified for the week.

Thanks by Strengths

Encourage people to express their thanks in ways that take advantage of their strengths. For example, my daughter is very artistic, and she can also be very shy. So rather than forcing her to walk up to a distant relative who just gave her a birthday present and mumble an insincere "Thanks," I can encourage her to create a thank-you card for him. Over time, she will begin to have much more positive associations with expressing gratitude and be more willing to do it in the future.

"THANKS" AT A GLANCE

- "Thanks" is magical because it lets people know they are contributing to the lives of others—which is a deep psychological desire.
- Saying "thanks" helps to balance the "positivity ratio" of any relationship.
- Ingratitude can be a result of adaptation.

- Gratitude has surprising health benefits.
- Saying "thanks" can actually make you feel more grateful.
- There are five components of an effective "thanks": be timely, compliment the attributes of the benefactor, recognize the intent of the benefactor, recognize the cost to the benefactor, and articulate the benefits you have received.
- Great leaders not only say "thanks," they create a "thanks culture" within the community of people around them.

WORDS MATTER BECAUSE CONNECTION MATTERS

We must never forget that words are powerful. After all, it was language that got us to the top of the food chain in the first place. In today's world, it will again be our words that get us to the top of our own personal food chain at work and in life.

Communication skills are more powerful than any other skill we can develop. Words inspire. Words sell. Words connect. In fact, subscribers to the *Harvard Business Review* rated the ability to communicate "the most important fact in making an executive promotable"—more important than ambition, education, hard work, and even technical skill.

Tragically, communication skills are disappearing at an alarming rate. Whether or not this is due to increased technology use and decreased face-to-face interactions, research has shown that we care less about each other and we are more narcissistic than at any point in recorded human history. We spend an average of seven and a half hours per day staring at a screen. Our desire to connect is becoming extinct.

Now that science has allowed us a glimpse into how our words *really* affect the brains of those around us, we can make wiser choices and begin to form more effective connections. We have the tools. Many of them are laid out in this volume. The only question is, are we willing to use them?

I believe that if solutions to the world's biggest and most pressing problems are ever discovered, they are likely to begin with an increase in human connection. When people come together, magical things happen. That's why the world needs more people who know how to drive others to action. We need leaders who can motivate, engage, influence, and inspire. Most important, we need more people who know how to use the power of words to bridge differences and connect with those around them.

Connection is what's really important. At the end of our lives, we will look back most fondly at the deep connections we've made and the relationships we've had.

That's why most people would agree that while it's possible to accumulate too much stuff in this world, it is impossible to accumulate too much human connection.

Human connection: now that's real magic.

ACKNOWLEDGMENTS

"Thanks" is quite possibly my favorite word. There is something beautiful about the magic it gives to both the person who hears it and the person who speaks it. I know that with all the people I have to thank for this book, I will be receiving gratitude benefits for a long time to come.

First, an extra-special thanks to my wife, Katie, and daughters, Chloe and Sophie, for their relentless love and support—even when the spotlight is off and my words are clumsy and decidedly un-magical. You inspire me more than you know.

To my agent, Giles Anderson, and his team for not only immediately seeing the diamond in the rough, but also working tirelessly with me to help polish it. Without his efforts to perfect and promote, it is certain that you wouldn't be holding this book in your hands right now.

To my editor, Jeanette Shaw, for treating my manuscript with such patience and respect. Her amazing ability to hew away the rough, and yet still let an author's voice come through, is the sole reason this book is readable.

To anyone who contributed content and insights, with a special nod to Jeffrey Froh, David Frees, Kenton Knepper, and Monica Cornetti. You all had such infectious enthusiasm for your respective areas of expertise. Thank you for your time and your talent.

To John Duff, and everyone else at Prentice Hall Press, for immediately catching the vision and standing behind this book 100 percent.

To my close friends and business partners Kennedy and Costas, for their tireless encouragement and endless brainstorming sessions. I respect you guys like you wouldn't believe.

To Cameron, for helping to keep my business afloat while I was off researching and writing. I've known you for a long time, and as a father myself, I'm certain that yours would be proud.

To the first humans I've ever observed, as well as my first audiences: Mom, Dad, Chris, Voo, Nana, and the rest of my family and friends. Thanks for planting seeds in my life and standing guard as they grew.

Finally, to you, for caring about human connection enough to make an improvement in your own communication skills. May your words motivate, engage, and influence in ways that you never thought possible!

Tim David has been a professional magician and mentalist since the age of nineteen, giving as many as three hundred live performances per year. He continues to practice and teach magic and mentalism, and in 2010 he was named the "Top Mentalist in North America." His popular YouTube channel receives over a hundred thousand views per month, and his students hail from more than seventy countries around the world.

Tim is currently focused on helping people become more effective and influential communicators. He presents more than one hundred keynotes and trainings each year, in addition to his audio programs, e-books, and online programs. Visit him at MagicWordsBook.com to read his blog and watch his videos, and follow him on Twitter @timdavidmagic.

He lives with his wife and children in Massachusetts.